# GMAT™
### Focus Edition

# Where do you see yourself in 6 weeks?

You can prep for the GMAT Focus Edition in less time than it takes to catch up on your favorite television shows. Get your FREE 6-Week Study Planner: **mba.com/6-weeks**

- **Start** your prep on the right foot
- **Track** your progress as you learn
- **Keep focused** on your business school journey
- **Gain tools and tips** to achieve your dream score

# GMAT™
## Focus Edition

For the GMAT™ Focus Edition

# GMAT™ Official Guide Data Insights Review

## 2023 – 2024

*Add additional Data Insights questions to your practice.*

**The only source of real GMAT questions**

**What's Included:**
- ✓ Over 200 Practice Questions
- ✓ Data Insights Review Chapter (New Section)
- ✓ Answer Explanations

**Plus! Online Exclusive:**
- ✓ **Mobile App** – Study on the Go
- ✓ Flashcards
- ✓ Track Your Progress

📖 Book + 💻 Online + 📱 Mobile

 mba.com

GMAT™ Official Prep

## GMAT™ Official Guide Data Insights Review 2023–2024

# Table of Contents

Dear GMAT™ Test Taker,

Thank you for your interest in graduate management education. Today more than 7,700 graduate programs around the world use the GMAT exam to establish their MBA, business master's, and other graduate-level management degree programs as hallmarks of excellence. Seven out of ten candidates apply to business school with their GMAT exam score.*

By using the *GMAT™ Official Guide* to prepare for the GMAT Focus Edition, you're taking a very important step toward achieving your goals and pursuing admission to the MBA or business master's program that is the best fit for you.

The *GMAT™ Official Guide Data Insights Review 2023–2024*, is designed to help you prepare for and build confidence to do your best on exam day. It's the only guide that features real GMAT questions published by the Graduate Management Admission Council (GMAC™), the makers of the GMAT exam. This guide and the other print and digital GMAT™ Official Prep products available at mba.com will give you the confidence to achieve your personal best on the GMAT exam and launch or reinvigorate a rewarding career.

For 70 years, the GMAT exam has helped candidates like you demonstrate their command of the skills needed for success in the classroom and showcase to schools their commitment to pursuing a graduate business degree. Schools use and trust the GMAT exam as part of their admissions process because it's a proven predictor of classroom success and your ability to excel in your chosen program.

The mission of GMAC is to ensure no talent goes undiscovered. We are driven to provide you with the tools and information you need to guide you through your journey in graduate management education, continuously improve the GMAT exam, and help you find and connect with the best-fit schools and programs for you.

We applaud your commitment to educational success and wish you the best on all your future educational and professional endeavors.

Sincerely,

Joy J. Jones
CEO, Graduate Management Admission Council

---

*Top 100 *Financial Times* full-time MBA programs

# GMAT™ Official Guide
# Data Insights Review 2023–2024

# 1.0   What Is the GMAT™ Exam?

# 1.0 What Is the GMAT™ Exam?

The Graduate Management Admission Test™ (GMAT™) is used in admissions decisions by more than 7,700 graduate management programs at about 2,400 business schools worldwide. It helps both you and these schools gauge how well you can do in graduate-level management studies. Unlike undergraduate grades and courses, whose meanings vary across regions and institutions, your GMAT scores are a standardized, statistically valid, and reliable measure of how well you are likely to do in the core courses of a graduate management program. This guide is for the **GMAT™ Focus Edition**.

The exam has three sections, which test your Verbal Reasoning, Quantitative Reasoning, and Data Insights skills. These skills include critical thinking, data analysis, and problem-solving, which all call for complex judgments. Management faculty and admissions professionals have found that incoming graduate students need these skills. And employers worldwide need their professional staff to have these skills as well.

This chapter gives more details about the GMAT Focus Edition below. You will take the exam on a computer either online or at a test center, always in English. It is not a test of business knowledge, subject mastery, English vocabulary, or advanced computing skills. Nor does it measure other factors helpful in business, such as job experience, leadership ability, motivation, or social skills. Your GMAT score is meant to be an objective, numeric measure of your ability and potential for success. Business schools will use it as part of their holistic admissions processes, which may also consider recommendation letters, essays, interviews, work experiences, and other signs of social and emotional intelligence as well as leadership.

# 1.1 Why Take the GMAT Exam?

Taking the exam helps you stand out as an applicant and show you're ready for and committed to graduate management education. Schools use GMAT scores in choosing the most qualified applicants. They know an applicant who has taken the exam is serious about earning a graduate business degree, and they know the exam scores reliably predict how well applicants can do in graduate business programs.

No matter how you do on the exam, you should contact schools that interest you to learn more about them and to ask how they use GMAT scores and other criteria in admissions decisions. School admissions offices, websites, and publications are key sources of information when you are researching business schools. Note that schools' published GMAT scores are averages of the scores of their admitted students, not minimum scores needed for admission.

## Myth -vs- FACT

**M –** If I don't get a high GMAT score, I won't get into my top-choice schools.

**F –** There are great schools for students with any GMAT score.

Few people taking the GMAT exam will get a perfect score of 805, yet many will get into top business-school programs around the world. Admissions officers will use GMAT scores as one factor in admissions decisions along with undergraduate records, application essays, interviews, letters of recommendation, and other information. Visit Program Finder on **mba.com** to learn which programs and schools are right for you.

To learn more about the exam, test preparation materials, registration, and how to use your GMAT scores in applying to business schools, please visit **mba.com/gmatfocus**.

# 1.2 GMAT™ Focus Edition Format

The GMAT™ Focus Edition has three separately timed sections (see the table on the following page). The Data Insights section includes multiple-choice questions along with other kinds of graphical and data analysis questions. The Quantitative Reasoning section and the Verbal Reasoning section have only multiple-choice questions.

All three GMAT sections are computer adaptive. This means the test chooses from a large bank of questions to adjust itself to your ability level, so you will not get many questions that are too hard or too easy for you. The first question will be of medium difficulty. As you answer each question, the computer uses your answer, along with your responses to earlier questions, to choose the next question with the right difficulty level.

Computer-adaptive tests get harder as you answer more questions right. But getting a question that seems easier than the last one doesn't always mean your last answer was wrong. The test must ask you many types of questions on different subjects, so it will not always give you a question of the perfect difficulty level.

A new feature in the GMAT is a bookmark you can use to mark any questions you feel unsure about during the exam. Another new feature lets you review and edit your answers at the end of each section. You can review and edit answers even to questions you have not bookmarked, but bookmarking a question helps you find it again quickly. You can bookmark as many questions as you like. You can review all questions whether or not they are bookmarked, but you can only change your answers to three questions per section. You must finish all your bookmarking, reviewing, and editing within each section's time limit. No extra time is given to use these new features.

Because the computer uses your answers to choose your next question, you cannot skip questions. But at the end of each section, you can go back, review all questions, and edit your answers for up to three questions. If you don't know how to answer a question, try to rule out as many wrong answer choices as possible. Then pick the answer choice you think is best.

Though each test taker gets different questions, the mix of question types is always the same. Your score depends on the difficulty and statistical traits of the questions you answer, as well as on which of your answers are right. By adapting to each test taker, the exam can accurately and efficiently gauge a full range of skill levels, from very high to very low.

The practice questions in this book and the online question bank accessed via **mba.com/my-account** are formatted and presented differently than questions on the actual exam. The practice questions are organized by question type and from easiest to hardest. But on the test, you may see different types of questions in any order within each section.

---

### Myth -vs- **FACT**

**M** – **Getting an easier question means I answered the last one wrong.**

**F** – **Worrying that a question seems too easy isn't helpful.**

Many factors may make the questions easier or harder, so don't waste time worrying if some questions seem easy.

To make sure every test taker gets equivalent content, the test gives specific numbers of questions of each type and about each kind of subject. But sometimes no available question perfectly meets these constraints. In this case, the test chooses the best available question, which may be slightly harder or easier than your next question would normally be. Also, remember you will be stronger in some subjects than in others. Since the test covers the same kinds of subjects for everyone, some items may be harder or easier for you than for other test takers.

Here are six things to know about GMAT questions:

(1)  The computer screen shows only one question or question prompt at a time, except for some types of Data Insights questions.

(2)  Radio buttons, rather than letters, mark the answer choices for multiple-choice questions.

(3)  The Data Insights section gives questions of different types in random order.

(4)  You must choose an answer and confirm your choice before moving on to the next question.

(5)  You can bookmark questions to remind yourself to review them at the end of the section.

(6)  Once you answer all of a section's questions, you may revisit any questions, whether bookmarked or not, and edit up to three answers in the section.

| Format of the GMAT™ Focus Edition | | |
|---|---|---|
| | Questions | Timing |
| **Data Insights**<br>Data Sufficiency<br>Multi-Source Reasoning<br>Table Analysis<br>Graphics Interpretation<br>Two-Part Analysis | 20 | 45 min. |
| **Quantitative Reasoning** | 21 | 45 min. |
| **Verbal Reasoning**<br>Reading Comprehension<br>Critical Reasoning | 23 | 45 min. |
| | Total Time | 135 min. |

On exam day, right before you start the exam, you can choose any order in which you will take the three sections. For example, you can choose to start with Verbal Reasoning, then do Quantitative Reasoning, and end with Data Insights. Or, you can choose to do Data Insights first, followed by Verbal Reasoning and then Quantitative Reasoning. Between sections, you can take one optional ten-minute break after either the first section or the second section.

# 1.3 What Is the Test Experience Like?

You can take the exam either online or at a test center—whichever you prefer. You may feel more comfortable at home with the online delivery format. Or you may prefer the uninterrupted, secure environment of a test center. It is your choice. Both options have the same content, structure, optional ten-minute break, scores, and score scales.

**At the Test Center:** Over 700 test centers worldwide administer the GMAT exam under standardized conditions. Each test center has proctored testing rooms with individual computer workstations that let you take the exam in a peaceful, quiet setting, with some privacy. You must not take notes or scratch paper into the testing room, but you will get an erasable notepad and marker to use during the test. To learn more about exam day, visit mba.com/gmatfocus.

**Online:** The GMAT exam delivered online is proctored remotely, so you can take it in the comfort of your home or office. You will need a quiet workspace with a desktop or laptop computer that meets minimum system requirements, a webcam, and a reliable internet connection. For more information about exam day, visit **mba.com/gmatfocus**.

To learn more about available accommodations for the exam, visit **mba.com/accommodations**.

# 1.4 What Is the Test Content Like?

The GMAT exam measures several types of analytical reasoning. The Data Insights section asks you to use diverse reasoning skills to solve realistic problems involving data. It also asks you to interpret and combine data from different sources and in different formats to reach conclusions. The Quantitative Reasoning section gives you basic arithmetic and algebra problems. Some are abstract, while others are realistic word problems.

The test questions are about various subjects, but the exam tells you everything you need to know to answer the questions. You do not need detailed outside knowledge of the subjects. The exam does not test business knowledge, vocabulary, or advanced computer skills. You will need basic math and English skills to do well on the test, but it mainly measures analytical and critical thinking skills.

## *Myth* -vs- **FACT**

**M** – **My GMAT score does not predict my success in business school.**

**F** – **False. The GMAT exam measures your critical thinking skills, which you will need in business school and your career.**

Hundreds of studies across hundreds of schools have proven the GMAT's validity. Together, these studies have shown that performance on the GMAT predicts success in business school even better than undergraduate grades do.

The exam measures how well you reason, solve problems, and analyze data. Some employers may even use the exam to judge your skills in these areas. Even if your program does not require GMAT scores, you can stand out from the crowd by doing well on the exam to show you have the skills to succeed in business school.

# 1.5 Data Insights Section

The GMAT Data Insights section highlights skills that today's business managers need to analyze intricate data and solve complex problems. It tests how well you can assess multiple sources and types of information—graphic, numeric, and verbal—as they relate to one another. It also tests how well you can analyze a practical math problem to tell if enough data is given to solve it. This section asks you to use math, data analysis, and verbal reasoning to analyze complex problems and solve related problems together.

The Data Insights section has five types of questions:

- Multi-Source Reasoning
- Table Analysis
- Graphics Interpretation
- Two-Part Analysis
- Data Sufficiency

Data Insights questions may require math, data analysis, verbal reasoning, or all three. You will have to interpret graphs and sort data tables to answer some questions, but you won't need advanced statistics or spreadsheet skills. For both online and test center exam delivery, you will have access to an on-screen calculator with basic functions for the Data Insights section, but *not* for the Quantitative Reasoning section.

In this book, Chapter 4, "Data Insights Review," reviews the basic data analysis skills you need to answer Data Insights questions. Chapter 5, "Data Insights," explains the Data Insights question types and gives test-taking tips.

For practice questions of each type, with full answer explanations, access the Online Question Bank by going to **mba.com/my-account** and using your unique access code on the inside front cover of this book.

# 1.6 Quantitative Reasoning Section

The GMAT Quantitative Reasoning section measures how well you solve math problems and interpret graphs. All questions in this section require solving problems using basic arithmetic, algebra, or both. Some are practical word problems, while others are pure math.

# 1.7 Verbal Reasoning Section

The GMAT Verbal Reasoning section measures how well you reason, understand what you read, and evaluate arguments. The Verbal Reasoning section includes passages about many topics. Neither the passages nor the questions assume you already know much about the topics discussed. Mingled throughout the section are multiple-choice questions of two main types: Reading Comprehension and Critical Reasoning.

# 1.8 How Are Scores Calculated?

The Verbal Reasoning, Quantitative Reasoning, and Data Insights sections are each scored on a scale from 60 to 90, in 1-point increments. You will get four scores: a Data Insights section score, a Verbal Reasoning section score, a Quantitative Reasoning section score, and a Total GMAT Score based on your three section scores. The Total GMAT Score ranges from 205 to 805. Your scores depend on:

- Which questions you answered right
- How many questions you answered
- Each question's difficulty and other statistical characteristics

An algorithm finds your scores based on the factors above. After you answer easier questions correctly, you will get harder questions to answer, letting you earn a higher score. The computer calculates your scores after you finish the exam or when your time runs out.

The following table shows the different types of scores, the scales, and the increments.

| Type of Score | Scale | Increments |
|---|---|---|
| Total Score | 205–805 | 10 |
| Quantitative Reasoning | 60–90 | 1 |
| Verbal Reasoning | 60–90 | 1 |
| Data Insights | 60–90 | 1 |

Your GMAT scores are valid for five years from your exam date. Your Total GMAT Score includes a predicted percentile ranking, which shows the percentage of tests taken with scores lower than your score. Visit **mba.com** to view the most recent predicted percentile rankings tables.

# 2.0  How to Prepare

# 2.0 How to Prepare

## 2.1 How Should I Prepare for the Test?

The GMAT™ Focus Edition has several unique question formats. You should at least know about the test format and these question formats before you take the test. Because the exam is timed, you should also try answering the practice questions in this book. By practicing, you'll learn to pace yourself so that you can finish each section during the exam. You'll also learn about the question formats and the skills you need.

Because the exam assesses reasoning rather than knowledge, memorizing facts probably won't help you. You don't need to study advanced math, but you should know some basic arithmetic and algebra. Likewise, you don't need to study advanced vocabulary words, but you should know English well enough to understand writing at an undergraduate level.

> ### Myth -vs- FACT
>
> **M –** **You need advanced math skills to get a high GMAT score.**
>
> **F –** **The exam measures your reasoning ability rather than your advanced math skills.**
>
> The exam only requires basic math. You should review the math skills in chapter 3 of this guide and in the *GMAT™ Official Guide Quantitative Review 2023–2024*. GMAT Quantitative Reasoning questions are challenging mainly because of the reasoning skills needed to solve the problems, not the underlying math skills.

## 2.2 Getting Ready for Exam Day

Whether you take the test online or in a test center, knowing what to expect will help you feel confident and succeed.

**Test Center**

While checking into a test center, be ready to:

- Show proper identification.

- Give your palm vein scan (where permitted by law).

- Give your digital signature to show that you understand and agree to the Test-Taker Rules and Agreement.

- Have a digital photograph taken.

For more information visit **mba.com/gmatfocus**.

**Online**

At least a day before you take your exam online:

- Check your computer—make sure your computer meets the minimum system requirements to run the exam.

- Prepare your workspace—find a quiet place to take your exam, clean your workspace, and remove all objects except your computer and whiteboard.

- Plan ahead—be ready to begin checking in 30 minutes before your scheduled exam time.

For more information visit **mba.com/gmatfocus**.

## 2.3 How to Use the *GMAT™ Official Guide Data Insights Review 2023–2024*

The *GMAT™ Official Guide Data Insights Review* is designed for those who have completed the Data Insights questions in the *GMAT™ Official Guide 2023–2024* and are looking for additional practice questions, as well as those who are interested in practicing only the Data Insights questions. Questions are organized by difficulty level from easy to hard, so if you are new to studying, we recommend starting at the beginning of each chapter and working your way through the questions sequentially. Some "easy" questions may seem hard to you, and some "hard" questions may seem easy. This is common. Different questions often seem harder to some people and easier to others.

You may also find the questions in this book generally easier or harder than questions you see on the Official Practice Exams or the actual exam. This is expected because, unlike the Official Practice Exams and the actual exam, this guidebook doesn't adjust to your abilities. In this book, about a third of the practice questions are easy, a third are medium, and a third are hard. However, on the actual exam and the Official Practice Exams, you probably won't find such an even mix of difficulty levels. Also, the proportions of questions about different content areas in this book don't reflect the proportions in the actual exam. To find questions of a specific type and difficulty level (for example, easy arithmetic questions), use the index of questions in chapter 6.

**TIP**

Since the exam is given on a computer, we suggest you practice the questions in this book using the **Online Question Bank** accessed via **mba.com/my-account**. It includes all the questions in this book, and it lets you create practice sets and track your progress more easily. The Online Question Bank is also available on your mobile device through the GMAT™ Official Practice mobile app. To access the Online Question Bank on your mobile device, first, create an account at **mba.com**, and then sign into your account on the mobile app.

## 2.4 How to Use Other GMAT Official Prep Products

We recommend using our other GMAT Official Prep products along with this guidebook.

- **For a realistic simulation of the exam:** GMAT™ Official Practice Exams 1–6 are the only practice exams that use real exam questions along with the scoring algorithm, user interface, and online whiteboard tool from the real exam. The first two practice exams are free to all test takers at **mba.com/gmatprep**.

- **For more practice questions:** *GMAT™ Official Guide Verbal Review 2023–2024, GMAT™ Official Guide Quantitative Review 2023–2024* offer more practice questions not included in this book.

For the best results:

1. Learn about the exam and the question types by reading the *GMAT™ Official Guide 2023–2024*.

2. Take the Diagnostic evaluation in the Online Question Bank (access via **mba.com/my-account**) to gauge your strengths and weaknesses.

3. Practice the questions in the *GMAT™ Official Guide 2023–2024*, focusing on skills you need to improve.

4. Take GMAT™ Focus Official Practice Exam 1. Do not worry about your score on this first practice exam! The goal is to become familiar with the exam and get a baseline score so that you can gauge your progress.

5. As you keep practicing, take more GMAT™ Focus Official Practice Exams to gauge your progress.

6. Before your actual GMAT exam, take a final GMAT™ Official Practice Exam to simulate the real test and see how you score.

The first two GMAT™ Official Practice Exams are in the free GMAT™ Official Starter Kit, which has free practice questions and is available to everyone with an **mba.com** account. You can buy GMAT™ Focus Official Practice Exams 3 to 6, more GMAT™ Focus Official Practice Questions, and other Official Prep products through **mba.com/gmatprep**.

# 2.5 Tips for Taking the Exam

Tips for answering questions of the different types are given later in this book. Here are some general tips to help you do your best on the test.

1. **Use your time wisely.**
   Although the exam stresses accuracy over speed, you should use your time wisely. On average, you have just under 2 minutes per Verbal Reasoning question, about 2 minutes, 9 seconds per Quantitative Reasoning question, and 2 minutes, 15 seconds per Data Insights question. Once you start the test, an on-screen clock shows how much time you have left. You can hide this display if you want, but by checking the clock periodically, you can make sure to finish in time.

2. **Before the actual exam, decide in what order to take the sections.**
   The exam lets you choose in which order you'll take the sections. Use the GMAT™ Official Practice Exams to practice and find your preferred order. No order is "wrong." Just practice each order and see which one works best for you.

3. **Try the practice questions ahead of time.**
   Timing yourself as you answer the practice questions can give you a sense of how long you will have for each question on the actual test, and whether you are answering them fast enough to finish in time.

> ## Myth -vs- **FACT**
>
> *M* – **Avoiding wrong answers is more important than finishing the test.**
>
> *F* – **Not finishing can lower your score a lot.**
>
> Pacing is important. If a question stumps you, just pick the answer choice that seems best and move on. If you guess wrong, the computer will likely give you an easier question, which you're more likely to answer right. Soon the computer will return to giving you questions matched to your ability. You can bookmark questions you get stuck on, then return to change up to three of your answers if you still have time left at the end of the section. But if you don't finish the section, your score will be reduced. Failing to answer five verbal questions, for example, could lower your score from the 91st percentile to the 77th percentile.

### TIP

After you've learned about all the question types, use the practice questions in this book and practice them online at **mba.com/my-account** to prepare for the actual test. Note that most types of Data Insights practice questions are available only online.

4.  **Study all test directions.**

    The directions explain exactly what you need to do to answer questions of each type. Study the directions so that you don't miss anything you need to know to answer properly. To review directions during the test, click on the Help icon. But note that your time spent reviewing directions counts against your available time for that section of the test.

5.  **Study each question carefully.**

    Before you answer a question, understand exactly what it says. Then pick the best answer choice. Never skim a question or the answer choices. Skimming may make you miss important details or nuances.

6.  **Do not spend too much time on any one question.**

    If finding the right answer is taking too long, try to rule out answer choices you know are wrong. Then pick the best of the remaining choices and move on to the next question.

    Not finishing sections or randomly guessing answers can lower your score significantly. As long as you've worked on each section, you will get a score even if you didn't finish one or more sections in time. You don't earn points for questions you never get to see.

7.  **Confirm your answers ONLY when you are ready to move on.**

    In the Quantitative Reasoning and Verbal Reasoning sections, once you choose your answer to a question, you are asked to confirm it. As soon as you confirm your response, the next question appears. You can't skip questions. In the Data Insights section, several questions based on the same prompt may appear at once. When more than one question is on a single screen, you can change your answers to any questions on that screen before moving on to the next screen. But until you've reached the end of the section, you can't navigate back to a previous screen to change any answers.

> ### Myth -vs- FACT
>
> **M – The first ten questions are critical, so you should spend the most time on them.**
>
> **F – All questions count.**
>
> The test uses each answered question to *initially* estimate how hard your questions should be. As you keep answering questions, the test adjusts by updating the estimate based on all your answers thus far. It then chooses questions that closely match its new estimate of your ability. Your final score depends on all your responses and on how hard all the questions you answered were. Taking extra time on the first ten questions won't game the system and might make you run out of time.

This book and other study materials from the Graduate Management Admission Council (GMAC) are the ONLY sources of real GMAT questions. All questions that appear or have appeared on the exam are copyrighted and owned by GMAC, which doesn't license them to be reprinted elsewhere. Accessing live GMAT questions in advance or sharing test content while or after you take the test is a serious violation. It could cause your scores to be canceled and schools to be notified. For serious violations, you may be banned from future testing, and other legal remedies may be pursued.

# 3.0    Math Review

# 3.0 Math Review

This chapter reviews the math you need to answer GMAT™ Quantitative Reasoning questions and some GMAT Data Insights questions. This is only a brief overview, so if you find unfamiliar terms, consult other resources to learn more.

Unlike some math problems you may have solved in school, GMAT math questions ask you to *apply* your math knowledge. For example, rather than asking you to list a number's prime factors to show you understand prime factorization, a GMAT question may ask you to *use* prime factorization and exponents to simplify an algebraic expression with a radical.

To prepare for the GMAT Quantitative Reasoning section and the Data Insights section, first review basic math to make sure you know enough to answer the questions. Then practice using GMAT questions from past exams.

Section 3.1, "Value, Order, and Factors," includes:

1. Numbers and the Number Line
2. Factors, Multiples, Divisibility, and Remainders
3. Exponents
4. Decimals and Place Value
5. Properties of Operations

Section 3.2, "Algebra, Equalities, and Inequalities," includes:

1. Algebraic Expressions and Equations
2. Linear Equations
3. Factoring and Quadratic Equations
4. Inequalities
5. Functions
6. Graphing
7. Formulas and Measurement Conversion

Section 3.3, "Rates, Ratios, and Percents," includes:

1. Ratio and Proportion
2. Fractions
3. Percents
4. Converting Decimals, Fractions, and Percents
5. Working with Decimals, Fractions, and Percents
6. Rate, Work, and Mixture Problems

Section 3.4, "Statistics, Sets, Counting, Probability, Estimation, and Series," includes:

1. Statistics
2. Sets
3. Counting Methods
4. Probability
5. Estimation
6. Sequences and Series

Section 3.5, Reference Sheets

# 3.1 Value, Order, and Factors

## 1. Numbers and the Number Line

**A.** All *real numbers* correspond to points on *the number line,* and all points on the number line represent real numbers.

The figure below shows the number line with labeled points standing for the real numbers $-\frac{3}{2}$, 0.2, and $\sqrt{2}$.

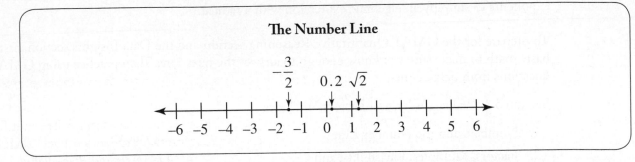

**The Number Line**

**B.** On a number line, points to the left of zero stand for *negative* numbers, and points to the right of zero stand for *positive* numbers. All real numbers except zero are either positive or negative.

**C.** For any two numbers on the number line, the number to the left is less than the number to the right. So, as the figure above shows, $-4 < -3 < -\frac{3}{2} < -1$, and $1 < \sqrt{2} < 2$.

**D.** If a number $n$ is between 1 and 4 on the number line, then $n > 1$ and $n < 4$; that is, $1 < n < 4$. If $n$ is "between 1 and 4, inclusive," then $1 \le n \le 4$.

**E.** The *absolute value* of a real number $x$, written as $|x|$, is $x$ if $x \ge 0$ and $-x$ if $x < 0$. A number's absolute value is the distance between that number and zero on the number line. Thus, $-3$ and $3$ have the same absolute value, since each is three units from zero on the number line. The absolute value of any nonzero number is positive.

*Examples:*

$|-5| = |5| = 5$, $|0| = 0$, and

$\left|\frac{-7}{2}\right| = \frac{7}{2}$.

For any real numbers $x$ and $y$, $|x + y| \le |x| + |y|$.

*Example:*

If $x = 10$ and $y = 2$, then $|x + y| = |12| = 12 = |x| + |y|$.

If $x = 10$ and $y = -2$, then $|x + y| = |8| = 8 < 12 = |x| + |y|$.

## 2. Factors, Multiples, Divisibility, and Remainders

**A.** An *integer* is any number in the set $\{\ldots -3, -2, -1, 0, 1, 2, 3, \ldots\}$. For any integer $n$, the numbers in the set $\{n, n + 1, n + 2, n + 3, \ldots\}$ are *consecutive integers*.

**B.** If $x$ and $y$ are integers and $x \neq 0$, then $x$ is a *divisor* or *factor* of $y$ if $y = xn$ for some integer $n$. Then $y$ is *divisible* by $x$ and is called a *multiple* of $x$.

> *Example:*
>
> Since $28 = (7)(4)$, both 4 and 7 are divisors or factors of 28.
>
> But 8 isn't a divisor or factor of 28, since $n$ isn't an integer if $28 = 8n$.

**C.** Dividing a positive integer $y$ by a positive integer $x$, and then rounding down to the nearest nonnegative integer, gives the *quotient* of the division.

To find the *remainder* of the division, multiply $x$ by the quotient, then subtract the result from $y$. The quotient and the remainder are the unique positive integers $q$ and $r$, respectively, such that $y = xq + r$ and $0 \leq r < x$.

> *Example:*
>
> When 28 is divided by 8, the quotient is 3 and the remainder is 4, because $28 = (8)(3) + 4$.

The remainder $r$ is 0 if and only if $y$ is *divisible* by $x$. Then $x$ is a divisor or factor of $y$, and $y$ is a multiple of $x$.

> *Example:*
>
> Since 32 divided by 8 has a remainder of 0, 32 is divisible by 8. So, 8 is a divisor or factor of 32, and 32 is a multiple of 8.

When a smaller integer is divided by a larger integer, the quotient is 0 and the remainder is the smaller integer.

> *Example:*
>
> When 5 is divided by 7, the quotient is 0 and the remainder is 5, since $5 = (7)(0) + 5$.

**D.** Any integer divisible by 2 is *even*; the set of even integers is $\{\ldots -4, -2, 0, 2, 4, 6, 8, \ldots\}$. Integers not divisible by 2 are *odd*, so $\{\ldots -3, -1, 1, 3, 5, \ldots\}$ is the set of odd integers. For any integer $n$, the numbers in the set $\{2n, 2n + 2, 2n + 4, \ldots\}$ are *consecutive even integers*, and the numbers in the set $\{2n + 1, 2n + 3, 2n + 5, \ldots\}$ are *consecutive odd integers*.

If a product of integers has at least one even factor, the product is even; otherwise, it's odd. If two integers are both even or both odd, their sum and their difference are even. Otherwise, their sum and their difference are odd.

E. A *prime* number is a positive integer with exactly two positive divisors, 1 and itself. That is, a prime number is divisible by no integer but itself and 1.

> *Example:*
>
> The first six prime numbers are 2, 3, 5, 7, 11, and 13.
>
> But 15 is not a prime number, because it has four positive divisors: 1, 3, 5, and 15.
>
> Nor is 1 a prime number, because it has only one positive divisor: itself.

Every integer greater than 1 is either prime or a product of a unique set of prime factors. A *composite number* is an integer greater than 1 that's not prime.

> *Example:*
>
> $14 = (2)(7)$, $81 = (3)(3)(3)(3)$, and
>
> $484 = (2)(2)(11)(11)$ are composite numbers.

## 3. Exponents

A. An expression of the form $k^n$ means the $n^{\text{th}}$ *power* of $k$, or $k$ raised to the $n^{\text{th}}$ power, where $n$ is the *exponent* and $k$ is the *base*.

B. A positive integer exponent shows how many instances of the base are multiplied together. That is, when $n$ is a positive integer, $k^n$ is the product of $n$ instances of $k$.

> *Examples:*
>
> $x^5$ is $(x)(x)(x)(x)(x)$; that is, the product in which $x$ is a factor 5 times and no other factors. We can also say $x^5$ is the $5^{\text{th}}$ power of $x$, or $x$ raised to the $5^{\text{th}}$ power.
>
> The $2^{\text{nd}}$ power of 2, also called 2 *squared*, is $2^2 = 2 \times 2 = 4$. The third power of 2, also called 2 *cubed*, is $2^3 = 2 \times 2 \times 2 = 8$.

Squaring a number greater than 1, or raising it to any power greater than 1, gives a larger number.

Squaring a number between 0 and 1 gives a smaller number.

> *Examples:*
>
> $3^2 = 9$, and $9 > 3$.
>
> $(0.1)^2 = 0.01$, and $0.01 < 0.1$.

**C.** A **square root** of a number $n$ is a number $x$ such that $x^2 = n$. Every positive number has two real square roots, one positive and the other negative. The positive square root of $n$ is written as $\sqrt{n}$ or $n^{\frac{1}{2}}$.

> *Example:*
>
> The two square roots of 9 are $\sqrt{9} = 3$ and $-\sqrt{9} = -3$.

For any $x$, the nonnegative square root of $x^2$ equals the absolute value of $x$; that is, $\sqrt{x^2} = |x|$. The square root of a negative number is not a real number and is called an **imaginary number**.

**D.** Every real number $r$ has exactly one real **cube root**, which is the number $s$ such that $s^3 = r$. The real cube root of $r$ is written as $\sqrt[3]{r}$ or $r^{\frac{1}{3}}$.

> *Examples:*
>
> Since $2^3 = 8$, $\sqrt[3]{8} = 2$.
>
> Likewise, $\sqrt[3]{-8} = -2$ because $(-2)^3 = -8$.

## 4. Decimals and Place Value

**A.** A **decimal** is a real number written as a series of digits, often with a period called a **decimal point**. The decimal point's position sets the **place values** of the digits.

> *Example:*
>
> The digits in the decimal 7,654.321 have these place values:
>
> | Thousands | | Hundreds | Tens | Ones or units | | Tenths | Hundredths | Thousandths |
> |---|---|---|---|---|---|---|---|---|
> | 7 | , | 6 | 5 | 4 | . | 3 | 2 | 1 |

**B.** In **scientific notation**, a decimal is written with only one nonzero digit to the decimal point's left, multiplied by a power of 10. To convert a number from scientific notation to regular decimal notation, move the decimal point by the number of places equal to the absolute value of the exponent on the 10. Move the decimal point to the right if the exponent is positive or to the left if the exponent is negative.

> *Examples:*
>
> In scientific notation, 231 is written as $2.31 \times 10^2$, and 0.0231 is written as $2.31 \times 10^{-2}$.
>
> To convert $2.013 \times 10^4$ to regular decimal notation, move the decimal point 4 places to the right, giving 20,130.
>
> Likewise, to convert $1.91 \times 10^{-4}$ to regular decimal notation, move the decimal point 4 places to the left, giving 0.000191.

**C.** To add or subtract decimals, line up their decimal points. If one decimal has fewer digits to the right of its decimal point than another, insert zeros to the right of its last digit.

> *Examples:*
>
> To add 17.6512 and 653.27, insert zeros to the right of the last digit in 653.27 to line up the decimal points when the numbers are in a column:
>
> $$\begin{array}{r} 17.6512 \\ + \, 653.2700 \\ \hline 670.9212 \end{array}$$
>
> Likewise for 653.27 minus 17.6512:
>
> $$\begin{array}{r} 653.2700 \\ -17.6512 \\ \hline 635.6188 \end{array}$$

**D.** Multiply decimals as if they were integers, then insert the decimal point in the product so that the number of digits to the right of the decimal point is the sum of the numbers of digits to the right of the decimal points in the numbers being multiplied.

> *Example:*
>
> To multiply 2.09 by 1.3, first multiply the integers 209 and 13 to get 2,717. Since $2 + 1 = 3$ digits to the right of the decimal points in 2.09 and 1.3, put 3 digits in 2,717 to the right of the decimal point to find the product:
>
> $$\begin{array}{r} 2.09 \quad \text{(2 digits to the right)} \\ \times \, 1.3 \quad \text{(1 digit to the right)} \\ \hline 627 \phantom{.0} \\ 2090 \phantom{.} \\ \hline 2.717 \quad (2+1=3 \text{ digits to the right}) \end{array}$$

**E.** To divide a number (the ***dividend***) by a decimal (the ***divisor***), move the divisor's decimal point to the right to make the divisor an integer. Then move the dividend's decimal point the same number of places to the right. Then divide as you would integers. The decimal point in the quotient goes directly above the decimal point in the new dividend.

*Example:*

To divide 698.12 by 12.4, first move the decimal points in both the divisor 12.4 and the dividend 698.12 one place to the right to make the divisor an integer. That is, replace 698.12/12.4 with 6981.2/124. Then do the long division normally:

$$
\begin{array}{r}
56.3 \\
124\overline{)6981.2} \\
\underline{620}\phantom{.2} \\
781 \\
\underline{744} \\
372 \\
\underline{372} \\
0
\end{array}
$$

## 5. Properties of Operations

Here are some basic properties of arithmetical operations for any real numbers $x$, $y$, and $z$.

**A.** Addition and Subtraction

$x + 0 = x = x - 0$

$x - x = 0$

$x + y = y + x$

$x - y = -(y - x) = x + (-y)$

$(x + y) + z = x + (y + z)$

If $x$ and $y$ are both positive, then $x + y$ is also positive.

If $x$ and $y$ are both negative, then $x + y$ is negative.

**B.** Multiplication and Division

$x \times 1 = x = \dfrac{x}{1}$

$x \times 0 = 0$

If $x \neq 0$, then $\dfrac{x}{x} = 1$

$\dfrac{x}{0}$ is undefined.

$xy = yx$

If $x \neq 0$ and $y \neq 0$, then $\dfrac{x}{y} = \dfrac{1}{\left(\frac{y}{x}\right)}$.

$(xy)z = x(yz)$

$xy + xz = x(y + z)$

If $y \neq 0$, then $\left(\dfrac{x}{y}\right) + \left(\dfrac{z}{y}\right) = \dfrac{(x + z)}{y}$.

If $x$ and $y$ are both positive, then $xy$ is also positive.

If $x$ and $y$ are both negative, then $xy$ is positive.

If $x$ is positive and $y$ is negative, then $xy$ is negative.

If $xy = 0$, then $x = 0$ or $y = 0$, or both.

**C.** Exponentiation

$x^1 = x$

$x^0 = 1$

If $x \neq 0$, then $x^{-1} = \frac{1}{x}$

$(x^y)^z = x^{yz} = (x^z)^y$

$x^{y+z} = x^y x^z$

If $x \neq 0$, then $x^{y-z} = \frac{x^y}{x^z}$.

$(xz)^y = x^y z^y$

If $z \neq 0$, then $\left(\frac{x}{z}\right)^y = \frac{x^y}{z^y}$.

If $z \neq 0$, then $x^{\frac{y}{z}} = (x^y)^{\frac{1}{z}} = \left(x^{\frac{1}{z}}\right)^y$.

# 3.2 Algebra, Equalities, and Inequalities

## 1. Algebraic Expressions and Equations

**A.** Algebra is based on arithmetic and on the concept of an **unknown quantity**. Letters like **x** or **n** are **variables** that stand for unknown quantities. Numerical expressions called **constants** stand for known quantities. A combination of variables, constants, and arithmetical operations is an **algebraic expression**.

Solving word problems often requires translating words into algebraic expressions. The table below shows how some words and phrases can be translated as math operations in algebraic expressions:

| 3.2 Translating Words into Math Operations | | | | |
|---|---|---|---|---|
| $x + y$ | $x - y$ | $xy$ | $\dfrac{x}{y}$ | $x^y$ |
| *x added to y* <br> *x increased by y* <br> *x more than y* <br> *x plus y* <br> *the sum of x and y* <br> *the total of x and y* | *x decreased by y* <br> *difference of x and y* <br> *y fewer than x* <br> *y less than x* <br> *x minus y* <br> *x reduced by y* <br> *y subtracted from x* | *x multiplied by y* <br> *the product of x and y* <br> *x times y* | *x divided by y* <br> *x over y* <br> *the quotient of x and y* <br> *the ratio of x to y* | *x to the power of y* <br> *x to the $y^{th}$ power* |
| | | If $y = 2$: <br> *double x* <br> *twice x* | If $y = 2$: <br> *half of x* <br> *x halved* | If $y = 2$: <br> *x squared* |
| | | If $y = 3$: <br> *triple x* | | If $y = 3$: <br> *x cubed* |

**B.** In an algebraic expression, a **term** is a constant, a variable, or a product of simpler terms that are each a constant or a variable. A variable in a term may be raised to an exponent. A term with no variables is a **constant term**. A constant in a term with one or more variables is a **coefficient**.

> *Example:*
>
> Suppose Pam has 5 more pencils than Fred has. If $F$ is the number of pencils Fred has, then the number of pencils Pam has is $F + 5$. The algebraic expression $F + 5$ has two terms: the variable $F$ and the constant term 5.

**C.** A **polynomial** is an algebraic expression that's a sum of terms and has exactly one variable. Each term in a polynomial is a variable raised to some power and multiplied by some coefficient. If the highest power a variable is raised to is 1, the expression is a **first degree** (or **linear**) **polynomial** in that variable. If the highest power a variable is raised to is 2, the expression is a **second degree** (or **quadratic**) **polynomial** in that variable.

> *Examples:*
>
> $F + 5$ is a linear polynomial in $F$, since the highest power of $F$ is 1.
>
> $19x^2 - 6x + 3$ is a quadratic polynomial in $x$, since the highest power of $x$ is 2.
>
> $\dfrac{3x^2}{(2x - 5)}$ is not a polynomial, because it's not a sum of powers of $x$ multiplied by coefficients.

**D.** You can simplify many algebraic expressions by factoring or combining **like** terms.

> *Examples:*
>
> The expression $6x + 5x$ is equivalent to $(6 + 5)x$, or $11x$.
>
> In the expression $9x - 3y$, 3 is a factor common to both terms: $9x - 3y = 3(3x - y)$.
>
> The expression $5x^2 + 6y$ has no like terms and no common factors.

**E.** In a fraction $\dfrac{n}{d}$, $n$ is the **numerator** and $d$ is the **denominator**. In an algebraic expression's numerator and denominator, you can divide out any common factors not equal to zero.

> *Example:*
>
> If $x \neq 3$, then $\dfrac{(x - 3)}{(x - 3)} = 1$.
>
> So $\dfrac{(3xy - 9y)}{(x - 3)} = \dfrac{3y(x - 3)}{(x - 3)} = 3y(1) = 3y$.

**F.** To multiply two algebraic expressions, multiply each term of one expression by each term of the other.

> *Example:*
>
> $$(3x - 4)(9y + x) = 3x(9y + x) - 4(9y + x)$$
> $$= 3x(9y) + 3x(x) - 4(9y) - 4(x)$$
> $$= 27xy + 3x^2 - 36y - 4x$$

**G.** To evaluate an algebraic expression, replace its variables with constants.

> *Example:*
>
> If $x = 3$ and $y = -2$, we can evaluate $3xy - x^2 + y$ as
>
> $3(3)(-2) - (3)^2 + (-2) = -18 - 9 - 2 = -29$.

**H.** An *algebraic equation* is an equation with at least one algebraic expression. An algebraic equation's *solutions* are the sets of assignments of constant values to its variables that make it true, or "satisfy the equation." An equation may have no solution, one solution, or more than one solution. For equations solved together, the solutions must satisfy all the equations at once. An equation's solutions are also called its *roots*. To confirm the roots are correct, you can substitute them into the equation.

**I.** Two equations with the same solution or solutions are *equivalent*.

> *Examples:*
>
> The equations $2 + x = 3$ and $4 + 2x = 6$ are equivalent, because each has the unique solution $x = 1$. Notice the second equation is the first equation multiplied by 2.
>
> Likewise, the equations $3x - y = 6$ and $6x - 2y = 12$ are equivalent, although each has infinitely many solutions. For any value given to $x$, giving the value $3x - 6$ to $y$ satisfies both these equations. For example, $x = 2$ with $y = 0$ is a solution to both equations, and so is $x = 5$ with $y = 9$.

## 2. Linear Equations

**A.** A *linear equation* has a linear polynomial on one side of the equals sign and either a linear polynomial or a constant on the other side—or can be converted to that form. A linear equation with only one variable is a *linear equation with one unknown*. A linear equation with two variables is a *linear equation with two unknowns*.

> *Examples:*
>
> $5x - 2 = 9 - x$ is a linear equation with one unknown.
>
> $3x + 1 = y - 2$ is a linear equation with two unknowns.

**B.** To solve a linear equation with one unknown (that is, to find what value of the unknown satisfies the equation), isolate the unknown on one side of the equation by doing the same operations on both sides. Adding or subtracting the same number from both sides of the equation doesn't change the equality. Likewise, multiplying or dividing both sides by the same nonzero number doesn't change the equality.

---

*Example:*

To solve the equation $\frac{5x-6}{3} = 4$, isolate the variable $x$ like this:

$$5x - 6 = 12 \quad \text{multiply both sides by 3}$$
$$5x = 18 \quad \text{add 6 to both sides}$$
$$x = \frac{18}{5} \quad \text{divide both sides by 5}$$

To check the answer $\frac{18}{5}$, substitute it for $x$ in the original equation to confirm it satisfies that equation:

$$\frac{\left(5\left(\frac{18}{5}\right) - 6\right)}{3} = \frac{(18 - 6)}{3} = \frac{12}{3} = 4$$

So $x = \frac{18}{5}$ is the solution.

---

**C.** If two linear equations with the same two unknowns are equivalent, they have infinitely many solutions, as in the example of the equivalent equations $3x - y = 6$ and $6x - 2y = 12$ in section 3.2.1.I above. But if two linear equations with the same two unknowns aren't equivalent, they have at most one solution.

Two linear equations with two unknowns can be solved in several ways. If in solving them you reach a trivial equation like $0 = 0$, the equations are equivalent and have infinitely many solutions. But if you reach a contradiction, the equations have no solution.

---

*Example:*

Consider the two equations $3x + 4y = 17$ and $6x + 8y = 35$. Note that $3x + 4y = 17$ implies $6x + 8y = 34$, contradicting the second equation. So, no values of $x$ and $y$ can satisfy both equations at once.

---

If neither a trivial equation nor a contradiction is reached, a unique solution can be found.

**D.** To solve two linear equations with two unknowns, you can use one of the equations to express one unknown in terms of the other unknown. Then substitute this result into the second equation to make a new equation with only one unknown. Next, solve this new equation. Substitute the value of its unknown into either of the original equations to find the value of the remaining unknown.

*Example:*

Let's solve these two equations for $x$ and $y$:

$$(1) \quad 3x + 2y = 11$$
$$(2) \quad x - y = 2$$

In equation (2), $x = 2 + y$. So, in equation (1), substitute $2 + y$ for $x$:

$$3(2 + y) + 2y = 11$$
$$6 + 3y + 2y = 11$$
$$6 + 5y = 11$$
$$5y = 5$$
$$y = 1$$

Since $y = 1$, we find $x - 1 = 2$, so $x = 2 + 1 = 3$.

**E.** Another way to remove one unknown and solve for $x$ and $y$ is to make the coefficients of one unknown the same in both equations (ignoring the sign). Then either add the equations or subtract one from the other.

*Example:*

Let's solve the equations:

$$(1) \quad 6x + 5y = 29 \text{ and}$$
$$(2) \quad 4x - 3y = -6$$

Multiply equation (1) by 3 and equation (2) by 5 to get

$$18x + 15y = 87 \text{ and}$$
$$20x - 15y = -30$$

Add the two equations to remove $y$. This gives us $38x = 57$, or $x = \frac{3}{2}$.

Substituting $\frac{3}{2}$ for $x$ in either original equation gives $y = 4$. To check these answers, substitute both values into both the original equations.

## 3. Factoring and Quadratic Equations

**A.** Some equations can be solved by *factoring*. To do this, first add or subtract to bring all the expressions to one side of the equation, with 0 on the other side. Then try to express the nonzero side as a product of factors that are algebraic expressions. When that's possible, setting any of these factors equal to 0 makes a simpler equation, because for any $x$ and $y$, if $xy = 0$, then $x = 0$ or $y = 0$ or both. The solutions of the simpler equations made this way are also solutions of the factored equation.

*Example:*

Factor to find the solutions of the equation $x^3 - 2x^2 + x = -5(x-1)^2$:

$$x^3 - 2x^2 + x + 5(x-1)^2 = 0$$
$$x(x^2 - 2x + 1) + 5(x-1)^2 = 0$$
$$x(x-1)^2 + 5(x-1)^2 = 0$$
$$(x+5)(x-1)^2 = 0$$
$$x + 5 = 0 \text{ or } x - 1 = 0$$
$$x = -5 \text{ or } x = 1.$$

So, $x = -5$  or  $x = 1$.

**B.** When factoring to solve equations with algebraic fractions, note that a fraction equals 0 if and only if its numerator equals 0 and its denominator doesn't.

*Example:*

Find the solutions of the equation $\dfrac{x(x-3)(x^2+5)}{x-4} = 0$

The numerator must equal 0: $x(x-3)(x^2+5) = 0$.

Thus, $x = 0$, or $x - 3 = 0$, or $x^2 + 5 = 0$. So, $x = 0$, or $x = 3$, or $x^2 + 5 = 0$.

But $x^2 + 5 = 0$ has no real solution, because $x^2 + 5 = 0$ for every real number $x$. So, the original equation's solutions are 0 and 3.

**C.** A ***quadratic equation*** has the standard form $ax^2 + bx + c = 0$, where $a$, $b$, and $c$ are real numbers and $a \neq 0$.

*Examples:*

$$x^2 + 6x + 5 = 0$$
$$3x^2 - 2x = 0, \text{ and}$$
$$x^2 + 4 = 0$$

**D.** Some quadratic equations are easily solved by factoring.

*Example (1):*

$$x^2 + 6x + 5 = 0$$
$$(x+5)(x+1) = 0$$
$$x + 5 = 0 \text{ or } x + 1 = 0$$
$$x = -5 \text{ or } x = -1$$

*Example (2):*

$$3x^2 - 3 = 8x$$
$$3x^2 - 8x - 3 = 0$$
$$(3x+1)(x-3) = 0$$
$$3x + 1 = 0 \text{ or } x - 3 = 0$$
$$x = -\frac{1}{3} \text{ or } x = 3$$

**E.** A quadratic equation has at most two real roots but may have just one or even no root.

> *Examples:*
>
> The equation $x^2 - 6x + 9 = 0$ can be written as $(x-3)^2 = 0$ or $(x-3)(x-3) = 0$. So, its only root is 3.
>
> The equation $x^2 + 4 = 0$ has no real root. Since any real number squared is greater than or equal to zero, $x^2 + 4$ must be greater than zero if $x$ is a real number.

**F.** An expression of the form $a^2 - b^2$ can be factored as $(a-b)(a+b)$.

> *Example:*
>
> We can solve the quadratic equation $9x^2 - 25 = 0$ like this:
> $$(3x - 5)(3x + 5) = 0$$
> $$3x - 5 = 0 \text{ or } x + 5 = 0$$
> $$x = \frac{5}{3} \text{ or } x = -\frac{5}{3}$$

**G.** If a quadratic expression isn't easily factored, we can still find its roots with the **quadratic formula**: If $ax^2 + bx + c = 0$ and $a \neq 0$, the roots are

$$x = \frac{-b + \sqrt{b^2 - 4ac}}{2a} \text{ and } x = \frac{-b - \sqrt{b^2 - 4ac}}{2a}$$

These roots are two distinct real numbers unless $b^2 - 4ac \leq 0$.

If $b^2 - 4ac = 0$, the two root expressions both equal $-\frac{b}{2a}$, so the equation has only one root.

If $b^2 - 4ac < 0$, then $\sqrt{b^2 - 4ac}$ is not a real number, so the equation has no real root.

## 4. Inequalities

**A.** An *inequality* is a statement with one of these symbols:

$\neq$ is not equal to

$>$ is greater than

$\geq$ is greater than or equal to

$<$ is less than

$\leq$ is less than or equal to

> *Example:*
>
> $5x - 3 < 9$ and $6x \geq y$

**B.** Solve a linear inequality with one unknown like you solve a linear equation: isolate the unknown on one side. As with an equation, the same number can be added to or subtracted from both sides of the inequality. And you can multiply or divide both sides by a positive number without changing the order of the inequality. However, multiplying or dividing an inequality by a negative number reverses the order of the inequality. Thus, $6 > 2$, but $(-1)(6) < (-1)(2)$.

---

*Example (1):*

To solve the inequality $3x - 2 > 5$ for $x$, isolate $x$:

$$3x - 2 > 5$$

$3x > 7$ (add 2 to both sides)

$x > \dfrac{7}{3}$ (divide both sides by 3)

*Example (2):*

To solve the inequality $\dfrac{5x - 1}{-2} < 3$ for $x$, isolate $x$:

$$\dfrac{5x - 1}{-2} < 3$$

$5x - 1 > -6$ (multiply both sides by $-2$)

$5x > -5$ (add 1 to both sides)

$x > -1$ (divide both sides by 5)

---

## 5. Functions

**A.** An algebraic expression in one variable can define a ***function*** of that variable. A function is written as a letter like $f$ or $g$ along with the variable in the expression. Function notation is a short way to express a value's substitution for a variable.

---

*Examples:*

(i) The expression $x^3 - 5x^2 + 2$ can define a function $f$ written as $f(x) = x^3 - 5x^2 + 2$.

(ii) The expression $\dfrac{2z + 7}{\sqrt{z + 1}}$ can define a function $g$ written as $g(z) = \dfrac{2z + 7}{\sqrt{z + 1}}$.

In these examples, the symbols "$f(x)$" and "$g(z)$" don't stand for products. Each is just a symbol for an algebraic expression, and is read "$f$ of $x$" or "$g$ of $z$."

The substitution of 1 for $x$ in the first expression can be written as $f(1) = -2$. Then $f(1)$ is called the "value of $f$ at $x = 1$."

Likewise, in the second expression the value of $g$ at $z = 0$ is $g(0) = 7$.

---

**B.** Once a function $f(x)$ is defined, think of $x$ as an input and $f(x)$ as the output. In any function, any one input gives at most one output. But different inputs can give the same output.

---

*Example:*

If $h(x) = |x + 3|$, then $h(-4) = 1 = h(-2)$.

---

**C.** The set of all allowed inputs for a function is the function's ***domain***. In the examples in section 3.2.5.A above, the domain of $f$ is the set of all real numbers, and the domain of $g$ is the set of all numbers greater than $-1$.

Any function's definition can restrict the function's domain. For example, the definition "$a(x) = 9x - 5$ for $0 \leq x \leq 10$" restricts the domain of $a$ to real numbers greater than or equal to 0 but less than or equal to 10. If the definition has no restrictions, the domain is the set of all values of $x$ that each give a real output when input into the function.

**D.** The set of a function's outputs is the function's **range**.

---

*Examples:*

(i) For the function $h(x) = |x + 3|$ in the example in section 3.2.5.B above, the range is the set of all numbers greater than or equal to 0.

(ii) For the function $a(x) = 9x - 5$ for $0 \leq x \leq 10$ defined in section 3.2.5.C above, the range is the set of every value $y$ such that $-5 \leq y \leq 85$.

---

## 6. Graphing

**A.** The figure below shows the rectangular **coordinate plane**. The horizontal line is the **x–axis** and the vertical line is the **y-axis**. These two axes intersect at the **origin**, called **O**. The axes divide the plane into four quadrants, I, II, III, and IV, as shown.

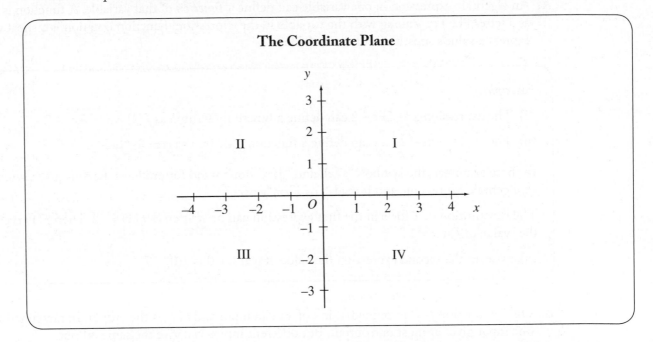

**The Coordinate Plane**

**B.** Any ordered pair $(x, y)$ of real numbers defines a point in the coordinate plane. The point's **x-coordinate** is the first number in this pair. It shows how far the point is to the right or left of the y-axis. If the x-coordinate is positive, the point is to the right of the y-axis. If it's negative, the point is to the left of the y-axis. If it's 0, the point is on the axis. The point's **y-coordinate** is the second number in the ordered pair. It shows how far the point is above or below the x-axis. If the y-coordinate is positive, the point is above the x-axis. If it's negative, the point is below the x-axis. If it's 0, the point is on the axis.

*Example:*

In the graph below, the $(x, y)$ coordinates of point $P$ are $(2,3)$. $P$ is 2 units to the right of the $y$-axis, so $x = 2$. Since $P$ is 3 units above the $x$-axis, $y = 3$.

Likewise, the $(x, y)$ coordinates of point $Q$ are $(-4,-3)$. The origin $O$ has coordinates $(0,0)$.

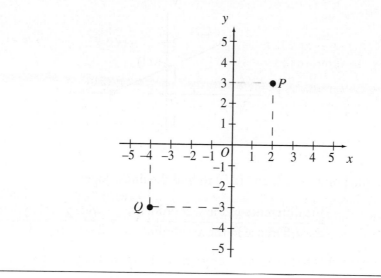

**C.** The coordinates of each point on a line in the coordinate plane satisfy a linear equation of the form $y = mx + b$ (or the form $x = a$ if the line is vertical).

In the equation $y = mx + b$, the coefficient $m$ is the line's **slope**, and the constant term $b$ is the line's **y-intercept**.

The $y$-intercept is the $y$-coordinate of the point where the line intersects the $y$-axis. Likewise, the **x-intercept** is the $x$-coordinate of the point where the line intersects the $x$-axis.

For any two points on the line, the slope is the ratio of the difference in their $y$-coordinates to the difference in their $x$-coordinates. To find the slope, subtract one point's $y$-coordinate from that of the others. Then subtract the former point's $x$-coordinate from the latter's—not the other way around!

If a line's slope is negative, the line slants down from left to right.

If its slope is positive, the line slants up.

If the slope is 0, the line is horizontal. A horizontal line's equation has the form $y = b$, since $m = 0$.

For a vertical line, the slope is not defined.

*Example:*

In the graph below, each point on the line satisfies the equation $y = -\frac{1}{2}x + 1$. To check this for the points $(-2,2)$, $(2,0)$, and $(0,1)$, substitute each point's coordinates for $x$ and $y$ in the equation.

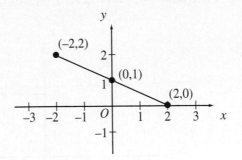

You can use the points $(-2,2)$ and $(2,0)$ to find the line's slope:

$$\frac{\text{the difference in the } y\text{-coordinates}}{\text{the difference in the } x\text{-coordinates}} = \frac{0 - 2}{2 - (-2)} = \frac{-2}{4} = -\frac{1}{2}.$$

The $y$-intercept is 1. That's the value of $y$ when $x$ is set to 0 in $y = -\frac{1}{2}x + 1$.

To find the $x$-intercept, set $y$ to 0 in the same equation:

$$-\frac{1}{2}x + 1 = 0$$
$$-\frac{1}{2}x = -1$$
$$x = 2.$$

Thus, the $x$-intercept is 2.

**D.** You can use the definition of slope to find the equation of a line through two points $(x_1,y_1)$ and $(x_2,y_2)$ with $x_1 \neq x_2$. The slope is $m = \frac{y_2 - y_1}{x_2 - x_1}$. Given the known point $(x_1,y_1)$ and the slope $m$, any other point $(x,y)$ on the line must satisfy the equation $m = \frac{(y - y_1)}{(x - x_1)}$, or equivalently $(y - y_1) = m(x - x_1)$. Using $(x_2,y_2)$ instead of $(x_1,y_1)$ as the known point gives an equivalent equation.

*Example:*

The graph below shows points $(-2,4)$ and $(3,-3)$.

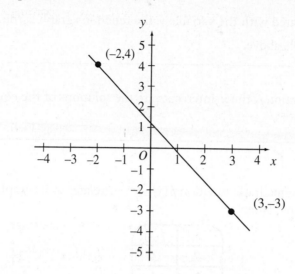

The line's slope is $\dfrac{(-3-4)}{(3-(-2))} = -\dfrac{7}{5}$. To find an equation of this line, let's use the point $(3,-3)$:

$$y - (-3) = \left(-\frac{7}{5}\right)(x - 3)$$

$$y + 3 = \left(-\frac{7}{5}\right)x + \frac{21}{5}$$

$$y = \left(-\frac{7}{5}\right)x + \frac{6}{5}$$

So, the $y$-intercept is $\dfrac{6}{5}$.

Find the $x$-intercept like this:

$$0 = -\frac{7}{5}x + \frac{6}{5}$$

$$\frac{7}{5}x = \frac{6}{5}$$

$$x = \frac{6}{7}$$

The graph shows both these intercepts.

**E.** If two linear equations with unknowns $x$ and $y$ have a unique solution, their graphs are two lines intersecting at the point that is the solution.

If two linear equations are equivalent, they both stand for the same line and have infinitely many solutions.

Two linear equations with no solution stand for parallel lines that don't intersect.

**F.** Graph any function $f(x)$ in the coordinate plane by equating $y$ with the function's value: $y = f(x)$. For any $x$ in the function's domain, the point $(x, f(x))$ is on the function's graph. For every point in the graph, the $y$-coordinate is the function's value at the $x$-coordinate.

*Example:*

Consider the function $f(x) = -\dfrac{7}{5}x + \dfrac{6}{5}$.

If $f(x)$ is equated with the variable $y$, the function's graph is the graph of the equation $y = -\dfrac{7}{5}x + \dfrac{6}{5}$ in the example above.

**G.** For any function $f$, the $x$-intercepts are the solutions of the equation $f(x) = 0$. The $y$-intercept is the value $f(0)$.

*Example:*

To see how a quadratic function $f(x) = x^2 - 1$ relates to its graph, let's plot some points $(x, f(x))$ in the coordinate plane:

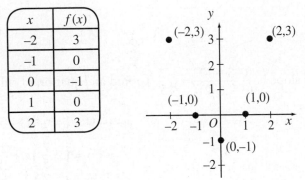

| $x$ | $f(x)$ |
|-----|--------|
| −2 | 3 |
| −1 | 0 |
| 0 | −1 |
| 1 | 0 |
| 2 | 3 |

The graph below shows all the points for $-2 \le x \le 2$:

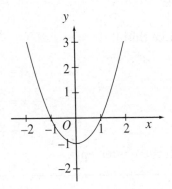

The roots of this equation $f(x) = x^2 - 1 = 0$ are $x = 1$ and $x = -1$. They match the $x$-intercepts, since $x$-intercepts are found by setting $y = 0$ and solving for $x$.

The $y$-intercept is $f(0) = -1$, because that's the value of $y$ for $x = 0$.

## 7. Formulas and Measurement Conversion

**A.** A *formula* is an algebraic equation whose variables have specific meanings. To use a formula, assign quantities to its variables to match these meanings.

---

*Example:*

In the physics formula $F = ma$, the variable $F$ stands for force, the variable $m$ stands for mass, and the variable $a$ stands for acceleration. The standard metric unit of force, the newton, is just enough force to accelerate a mass of 1 kilogram by 1 meter/second$^2$.

So, if we know a rock with a mass of 2 kilograms is accelerating at 5 meters/second$^2$, we can use the formula $F = ma$ by setting the variable $m$ to 2 kilograms, and the variable $a$ to 5 meters/second$^2$. Then we find that 10 newtons of force $F$ are pushing the rock.

Note: You don't need to learn physics formulas or terms like this to prepare for the GMAT, but some specific GMAT questions may give you the formulas and terms you need to solve them.

---

**B.** Any quantitative relationship between units of measure can be written as a formula.

---

*Examples:*

(i) Since 1 kilometer is 1,000 meters, the formula $m = 1000k$ can stand for the relationship between kilometers ($k$) and meters ($m$).

(ii) The formula $C = \frac{5}{9}(F - 32)$ can stand for the relationship between temperature measurements in degrees Celsius ($C$) and degrees Fahrenheit ($F$).

---

**C.** Except for units of time, a GMAT question that requires converting one unit of measure to another will give the relationship between those units.

---

*Example:*

A train travels at a constant 25 meters per second. How many kilometers does it travel in 5 minutes? (1 kilometer = 1,000 meters)

*Solution:* In 1 minute the train travels $(25)(60) = 1,500$ meters, so in 5 minutes it travels 7,500 meters. Since 1 kilometer = 1,000 meters, we find 7,500 meters = 7.5 kilometers.

---

# 3.3 Rates, Ratios, and Percents

## 1. Ratio and Proportion

**A.** The *ratio* of a number $x$ to a nonzero number $y$ may be written as $x : y$, or $\frac{x}{y}$, or $x$ to $y$. The order of a ratio's terms is important. Unless the absolute values of $x$ and $y$ are equal, $\frac{x}{y} \neq \frac{y}{x}$.

> *Examples:*
>
> The ratio of 2 to 3 may be written as 2:3, or $\frac{2}{3}$, or 2 to 3.
>
> The ratio of the number of months with exactly 30 days to the number of months with exactly 31 days is 4:7, not 7:4.

**B.** A *proportion* is an equation between two ratios.

> *Example:*
>
> 2:3 = 8:12 is a proportion.

**C.** One way to solve for an unknown in a proportion is to cross multiply, then solve the resulting equation.

> *Example:*
>
> To solve for $n$ in the proportion $\frac{2}{3} = \frac{n}{12}$, cross multiply to get $3n = 24$, then divide both sides by 3 to find $n = 8$.

**D.** Some word problems can be solved using ratios.

> *Example:*
>
> If 5 shirts cost a total of $44, then what is the total cost of 8 shirts at the same cost per shirt?
>
> *Solution:* If $c$ is the cost of the 8 shirts, then $\frac{5}{44} = \frac{8}{c}$. Cross multiplying gives $5c = 8 \times 44 = 352$, so $c = \frac{352}{5} = 70.4$. Thus, the 8 shirts cost a total of $70.40.

## 2. Fractions

**A.** In a fraction $\frac{n}{d}$, $n$ is the **numerator** and $d$ is the **denominator**. A fraction's denominator can never be 0, because division by 0 is undefined.

**B.** *Equivalent* fractions stand for the same number. To check whether two fractions are equivalent, divide each fraction's numerator and denominator by the largest factor common to that numerator and that denominator, their **greatest common divisor** (gcd). This is called **reducing each fraction to its lowest terms**. Two fractions are equivalent if and only if reducing each to its lowest terms makes them identical.

*Example:*

To check whether $\frac{8}{36}$ and $\frac{14}{63}$ are equivalent, first reduce each to its lowest terms. In the first fraction, 4 is the gcd of the numerator 8 and the denominator 36. Dividing both the numerator and the denominator of $\frac{8}{36}$ by 4 gives $\frac{2}{9}$. In the second fraction, 7 is the gcd of the numerator 14 and the denominator 63. Dividing both the numerator and the denominator of $\frac{14}{63}$ by 7 also gives $\frac{2}{9}$. Since reducing $\frac{8}{36}$ and $\frac{14}{63}$ to their lowest terms makes them identical, they're equivalent.

**C.** To add or subtract two fractions with the same denominator, just add or subtract the numerators, leaving the denominators the same.

*Examples:*

$\frac{3}{5} + \frac{4}{5} = \frac{3+4}{5} = \frac{7}{5}$ and

$\frac{5}{7} - \frac{2}{7} = \frac{5-2}{7} = \frac{3}{7}$

**D.** To add or subtract two fractions with different denominators, first express them as fractions with the same denominator.

*Example:*

To add $\frac{3}{5}$ and $\frac{4}{7}$, multiply the numerator and denominator of $\frac{3}{5}$ by 7 to get $\frac{21}{35}$. Then multiply the numerator and denominator of $\frac{4}{7}$ by 5 to get $\frac{20}{35}$. Since both fractions now have the same denominator 35, you can easily add them: $\frac{3}{5} + \frac{4}{7} = \frac{21}{35} + \frac{20}{35} = \frac{41}{35}$

**E.** To multiply two fractions, multiply their numerators, and also multiply their denominators.

*Example:*

$\frac{2}{3} \times \frac{4}{7} = \frac{2 \times 4}{3 \times 7} = \frac{8}{21}$

**F.** The *reciprocal* of a fraction $\frac{n}{d}$ is $\frac{d}{n}$ if $n$ and $d$ are not 0.

*Example:*

The reciprocal of $\frac{4}{7}$ is $\frac{7}{4}$

**G.** To divide by a fraction, multiply by its reciprocal.

> *Example:*
>
> $$\frac{2}{3} \div \frac{4}{7} = \frac{2}{3} \times \frac{7}{4} = \frac{14}{12} = \frac{7}{6}$$

**H.** A *mixed number* is written as an integer next to a fraction. It equals the integer plus the fraction.

> *Example:*
>
> The mixed number $7\frac{2}{3} = 7 + \frac{2}{3}$

**I.** To write a mixed number as a fraction, multiply the integer part of the mixed number by the denominator of the fractional part. Add this product to the numerator. Then put this sum over the denominator.

> *Example:*
>
> $$7\frac{2}{3} = \frac{(7 \times 3) + 2}{3} = \frac{23}{3}$$

## 3. Percents

**A.** The word *percent* means *per hundred* or *number out of 100.*

> *Example:*
>
> Saying that 37 percent, or 37%, of the houses in a city are painted blue means that 37 houses per 100 in the city are painted blue.

**B.** A percent may be greater than 100.

> *Example:*
>
> Saying that the number of blue houses in a city is 150% of the number of red houses means the city has 150 blue houses for every 100 red houses. Since 150:100 = 3:2, this is the same as saying the city has 3 blue houses for every 2 red houses.

**C.** A percent need not be an integer.

> *Example:*
>
> Saying that the number of pink houses in a city is 0.5% of the number of blue houses means the city has 0.5 of a pink house for every 100 blue houses. Since 0.5:100 = 1:200, this is the same as saying the city has 1 pink house for every 200 blue houses.
>
> Likewise, saying that the number of orange houses is 12.5% of the number of blue houses means the ratio of orange houses to blue houses is 12.5:100 = 1:8. Therefore, there is 1 orange house for every 8 blue houses.

## 4. Converting Decimals, Fractions, and Percents

**A.** Decimals can be rewritten as fractions or sums of fractions.

> *Examples:*
>
> $$0.321 = \frac{3}{10} + \frac{2}{100} + \frac{1}{1,000} = \frac{321}{1,000}$$
>
> $$0.0321 = \frac{0}{10} + \frac{3}{100} + \frac{2}{1,000} + \frac{1}{10,000} = \frac{321}{10,000}$$
>
> $$1.56 = 1 + \frac{5}{10} + \frac{6}{100} = \frac{156}{100}$$

**B.** To rewrite a percent as a fraction, write the percent number as the numerator over a denominator of 100. To rewrite a percent as a decimal, move the decimal point in the percent two places to the left and drop the percent sign. To rewrite a decimal as a percent, move the decimal point two places to the right, then add a percent sign.

> *Examples:*
>
> $$37\% = \frac{37}{100} = 0.37$$
>
> $$300\% = \frac{300}{100} = 3$$
>
> $$0.5\% = \frac{0.5}{100} = 0.005$$

**C.** To find a certain percent of a number, multiply the number by the percent expressed as a fraction or decimal.

> *Examples:*
>
> $20\% \text{ of } 90 = 90\left(\frac{20}{100}\right) = 90\left(\frac{1}{5}\right) = \frac{90}{5} = 18$
>
> $20\% \text{ of } 90 = 90(0.2) = 18$
>
> $250\% \text{ of } 80 = 80\left(\frac{250}{100}\right) = 80(2.5) = 200$
>
> $0.5\% \text{ of } 12 = 12\left(\frac{0.5}{100}\right) = 12(0.005) = 0.06$

## 5. Working with Decimals, Fractions, and Percents

**A.** To find the percent increase or decrease from one quantity to another, first find the amount of increase or decrease. Then divide this amount by the original quantity. Write this quotient as a percent.

> *Examples:*
>
> Suppose a price increases from $24 to $30. To find the percent increase, first find the amount of increase: $30 − $24 = $6. Divide this $6 by the original price of $24 to find the percent increase: $\frac{6}{24} = 0.25 = 25\%$.
>
> Now suppose a price falls from $30 to $24. The amount of decrease is $30 − $24 = $6. So, the percent decrease is $\frac{6}{30} = 0.20 = 20\%$.
>
> Notice the percent **increase** from 24 to 30 (25%) doesn't equal the percent **decrease** from 30 to 24 (20%).

A percent increase or decrease may be greater than 100%.

> *Example:*
>
> Suppose a house's price in 2018 was 300% of its price in 2003. By what percent did the price increase?
>
> *Solution:* If $n$ is the price in 2003, the percent increase is $\left|\frac{(3n - n)}{n}\right| = \left|\frac{2n}{n}\right| = 2$, or 200%.

**B.** A price discounted by *n* percent is $(100 - n)$ percent of the original price.

> *Example:*
>
> A customer paid $24 for a dress. If the customer got a 25% discount off the original price of the dress, what was the original price before the discount?
>
> *Solution:* The discounted price is $(100 - 25 = 75)\%$ of the original price. So, if *p* is the original price, $0.75p = \$24$ is the discounted price. Thus, $p = (\$24 / 0.75) = \$32$, the original price before the discount.

Two discounts can be combined to make a larger discount.

> *Example:*
>
> A price is discounted 20%. Then this reduced price is discounted another 30%. These two discounts together make an overall discount of what percent?
>
> *Solution:* If *p* is the original price, then $0.8p$ is the price after the first discount. The price after the second discount is $(0.7)(0.8) \, p = 0.56p$. The overall discount is $100\% - 56\% = 44\%$.

**C.** *Gross profit* equals revenues minus expenses, or selling price minus cost

> *Example:*
>
> A certain appliance costs a merchant $30. At what price should the merchant sell the appliance to make a gross profit of 50% of the appliance's cost?
>
> *Solution:* The merchant should sell the appliance for a price *s* such that $s - 30 = (0.5)(30)$. So, $s = \$30 + \$15 = \$45$.

**D.** *Simple annual interest* on a loan or investment is based only on the original loan or investment amount (the *principal*). It equals (principal) × (interest rate) × (time).

> *Example:*
>
> If $8,000 is invested at 6% simple annual interest, how much interest is earned after 3 months?
>
> *Solution:* Since the annual interest rate is 6%, the interest for 1 year is $(0.06)(\$8,000) = \$480$.
>
> A year has 12 months, so the interest earned in 3 months is $\left(\frac{3}{12}\right)(\$480) = \$120$.

E. **Compound interest** is based on the principal plus any interest already earned.

Compound interest over $n$ periods = (principal) × (1 + interest per period)$^n$ − principal.

---

*Example:*

If $10,000 is invested at 10% annual interest, compounded every 6 months, what is the balance after 1 year?

*Solution:* Since the interest is compounded every 6 months, or twice a year, the interest rate for each 6-month period is 5%, half the 10% annual rate. So, the balance after the first 6 months is 10,000 + (10,000)(0.05) = $10,500.

For the second 6 months, the interest is based on the $10,500 balance after the first 6 months. So, the balance after 1 year is 10,500 + (10,500)(0.05) = $11,025.

The balance after 1 year can also be written as $10{,}000 \times \left(1 + \dfrac{0.10}{2}\right)^2$ dollars.

---

F. To solve some word problems with percents and fractions, you can organize the information in a table.

---

*Example:*

In a production lot, 40% of the toys are red, and the rest are green. Half of the toys are small, and half are large. If 10% of the toys are red and small, and 40 toys are green and large, how many of the toys are red and large?

*Solution:* First make a table to organize the information:

|       | Red  | Green | Total |
|-------|------|-------|-------|
| Small | 10%  |       | 50%   |
| Large |      |       | 50%   |
| Total | 40%  | 60%   | 100%  |

Then fill in the missing percents so that the "Red" and "Green" percents in each row add up to that row's total, and the "Small" and "Large" percents in each column add up to that column's total:

|       | Red  | Green | Total |
|-------|------|-------|-------|
| Small | 10%  | 40%   | 50%   |
| Large | 30%  | 20%   | 50%   |
| Total | 40%  | 60%   | 100%  |

The number of large green toys, 40, is 20% of the total number of toys ($n$), so $0.20n = 40$. Thus, the total number of toys $n = 200$. So, 30% of the 200 toys are red and large. Since $(0.3)(200) = 60$, we find that 60 of the toys are red and large.

## 6. Rate, Work, and Mixture Problems

**A.** The distance an object travels is its average speed multiplied by the time it takes to travel that distance. That is, ***distance = rate × time.***

> *Example:*
>
> How many kilometers did a car travel in 4 hours at an average speed of 70 kilometers per hour?
>
> *Solution:* Since distance = rate × time, multiply 70 km/hour × 4 hours to find that the car went 280 kilometers.

**B.** To find an object's average travel speed, divide the total travel distance by the total travel time.

> *Example:*
>
> On a 600-kilometer trip, a car went half the distance at an average speed of 60 kilometers per hour (kph), and the other half at an average speed of 100 kph. The car didn't stop between the two halves of the trip. What was the car's average speed over the whole trip?
>
> *Solution:* First find the total travel time. For the first 300 kilometers, the car went at 60 kph, taking $\frac{300}{60} = 5$ hours. For the second 300 kilometers, the car went at 100 kph, taking $\frac{300}{100} = 3$ hours. So, the total travel time was 5 + 3 = 8 hours. The car's average speed was $\frac{600 \text{ kilometers}}{8 \text{ hours}} = 75$ kph. Notice the average speed was not $\frac{(60 + 100)}{2} = 80$ kph.

**C.** A ***work problem*** usually says how fast certain individuals work and asks you to find how fast they work together, or vice versa.

The basic formula for work problems is $\frac{1}{r} + \frac{1}{s} = \frac{1}{h}$, where $r$ is how long an amount of work takes a certain individual, $s$ is how long that much work takes a different individual, and $h$ is how long that much work takes both individuals working at the same time.

> *Example:*
>
> Suppose one machine takes 4 hours to make 1,000 bolts, and a second machine takes 5 hours to make 1,000 bolts. How many hours do both machines working at the same time take to make 1,000 bolts?
>
> *Solution:*
> $$\frac{1}{4} + \frac{1}{5} = \frac{1}{h}$$
> $$\frac{5}{20} + \frac{4}{20} = \frac{1}{h}$$
> $$\frac{9}{20} = \frac{1}{h}$$
> $$9h = 20$$
> $$h = \frac{20}{9} = 2\frac{2}{9}$$
>
> Working together, the two machines can make 1,000 bolts in $2\frac{2}{9}$ hours.

Use the same formula to find how long it takes one individual to do an amount of work alone.

*Example:*

Suppose Art and Rita both working at the same time take 4 hours to do an amount of work, and Art alone takes 6 hours to do that much work. Then how many hours does Rita alone take to do that much work?

*Solution:*

$$\frac{1}{6} + \frac{1}{R} = \frac{1}{4}$$

$$\frac{1}{R} = \frac{1}{4} - \frac{1}{6} = \frac{1}{12}$$

$$R = 12$$

Rita alone takes 12 hours to do that much work.

**D.** In *mixture problems*, substances with different properties are mixed, and you must find the mixture's properties.

*Example:*

If 6 kilograms of nuts that cost $1.20 per kilogram are mixed with 2 kilograms of nuts that cost $1.60 per kilogram, how much does the mixture cost per kilogram?

*Solution:* The 8 kilograms of nuts cost a total of 6($1.20) + 2($1.60) = $10.40. So, the cost per kilogram is $\frac{\$10.40}{8}$ = $1.30.

Some mixture problems use percents.

*Example:*

How many liters of a solution that is 15% salt must be added to 5 liters of a solution that is 8% salt to make a solution that is 10% salt?

*Solution:* Let $n$ be the needed number of liters of the 15% solution. The amount of salt in $n$ liters of 15% solution is $0.15n$. The amount of salt in the 5 liters of 8% solution is $(0.08)(5)$. These amounts add up to the amount of salt in the 10% mixture, which is $0.10(n + 5)$. So,

$$0.15n + 0.08(5) = 0.10(n + 5)$$

$$15n + 40 = 10n + 50$$

$$5n = 10$$

$$n = 2 \text{ liters}$$

So, 2 liters of the 15% salt solution must be added to the 8% solution to make the 10% solution.

# 3.4 Statistics, Sets, Counting, Probability, Estimation, and Series

## 1. Statistics

**A.** A common statistical measure is the *average* or *(arithmetic) mean,* a type of center for a set of numbers. The average or mean of $n$ numbers is the sum of the $n$ numbers divided by $n$.

*Example:*

The average of the 5 numbers 6, 4, 7, 10, and 4 is $\dfrac{(6 + 4 + 7 + 10 + 4)}{5} = \dfrac{31}{5} = 6.2$.

**B.** The *median* is another type of center for a set of numbers. To find the median of $n$ numbers, order the numbers from least to greatest. If $n$ is odd, the median is the middle number in the list. But if $n$ is even, the median is the average of the two middle numbers. The median may be less than, equal to, or greater than the mean of the same numbers.

*Example:*

To find the median of the 5 numbers 6, 4, 7, 10, and 4, order them from least to greatest: 4, 4, 6, 7, 10. The median is 6, the middle number in this list

The median of the 6 numbers 4, 6, 6, 8, 9, 12 is $\dfrac{(6 + 8)}{2} = 7$. But the mean of these 6 numbers is $\dfrac{(4 + 6 + 6 + 8 + 9 + 12)}{6} = \dfrac{45}{6} = 7.5$.

Often about half the numbers in a set are less than the median, and about half are greater than the median. But not always.

*Example:*

For the 15 numbers 3, 5, 7, 7, 7, 7, 7, 7, 8, 9, 9, 9, 9, 10, and 10, the median is 7. Only $\dfrac{2}{15}$ of the numbers are less than the median.

**C.** The *mode* of a list of numbers is the number that occurs most often in the list.

*Example:*

The mode of the list of numbers 1, 3, 6, 4, 3, 5 is 3, since 3 is the only number that occurs more than once in the list.

A list of numbers may have more than one mode.

> *Example:*
>
> The list 1, 2, 3, 3, 3, 5, 7, 10, 10, 10, 20 has two modes, 3 and 10.

**D.** There are many ways to measure how spread out or dispersed numerical data are. The simplest measure of dispersion is the ***range,*** which is the greatest value in the data minus the least value.

> *Example:*
>
> The range of the 5 numbers 11, 10, 5, 13, 21 is 21 − 5 = 16. Notice the range depends on only 2 of the numbers.

**E.** Another common measure of dispersion is the ***standard deviation.*** Generally, the farther the numbers spread away from the mean, the greater the standard deviation. To find the standard deviation of $n$ numbers:

(1) Find their arithmetic mean,

(2) Find the differences between the mean and each of the $n$ numbers,

(3) Square each difference,

(4) Find the average of the squared differences, and

(5) Take the nonnegative square root of this average.

> *Examples:*
>
> Let's use the table below to find the standard deviation of the 5 numbers 0, 7, 8, 10, 10, which have the mean 7.
>
> | $x$ | $x - 7$ | $(x - 7)^2$ |
> |:---:|:---:|:---:|
> | 0 | −7 | 49 |
> | 7 | 0 | 0 |
> | 8 | 1 | 1 |
> | 10 | 3 | 9 |
> | 10 | 3 | 9 |
> | | Total | 68 |
>
> The standard deviation is $\sqrt{\dfrac{68}{5}} \approx 3.7$
>
> The standard deviation depends on every number in the set, but more on those farther from the mean. This is why the standard deviation is smaller for a set of data grouped closer around its mean.
>
> As a second example, consider the numbers 6, 6, 6.5, 7.5, 9, which also have the mean 7. These numbers are grouped closer around the mean 7 than the numbers in the first example. That makes the standard deviation in this second example only about 1.1, far below the standard deviation of 3.7 in the first example.

**F.** How many times a value occurs in a data set is its *frequency* in the set. When different data values have different frequencies, a *frequency distribution* can help show how the values are distributed.

*Example:*

Consider this data set of 20 numbers:

$$-4 \quad 0 \quad 0 \quad -3 \quad -2 \quad -1 \quad -1 \quad 0 \quad -1 \quad -4$$
$$-1 \quad -5 \quad 0 \quad -2 \quad 0 \quad -5 \quad -2 \quad 0 \quad 0 \quad -1$$

We can show its frequency distribution in a table listing each data value $x$ and $x$'s frequency $f$:

| Data Value $x$ | Frequency $f$ |
|:---:|:---:|
| −5 | 2 |
| −4 | 2 |
| −3 | 1 |
| −2 | 3 |
| −1 | 5 |
| 0 | 7 |
| Total | 20 |

This frequency distribution table makes computing statistical measures easier:

Mean: $= \dfrac{(-5)(2) + (-4)(2) + (-3)(1) + (-2)(3) + (-1)(5) + (0)(7)}{20} = -1.6$

Median: −1 (the average of the 10th and 11th numbers)

Mode: 0 (the number that occurs most often)

Range: $0 - (-5) = 5$

Standard deviation: $\sqrt{\dfrac{(-5 + 1.6)^2(2) + (-4 + 1.6)^2(2) + \ldots + (0 + 1.6)^2(7)}{20}} \approx 1.7$

# 2. Sets

**A.** In math, a *set* is a collection of numbers or other things. The things in the set are its *elements*. A list of a set's elements in a pair of braces stands for the set. The list's order doesn't matter.

*Example:*

$\{-5, 0, 1\}$ is the same set as $\{0, 1, -5\}$. That is, $\{-5, 0, 1\} = \{0, 1, -5\}$.

**B.** The number of elements in a finite set $S$ is written as $|S|$.

> *Example:*
> $S = \{-5, 0, 1\}$ is a set with $|S| = 3$.

**C.** If all the elements in a set $S$ are also in a set $T$, then $S$ is a ***subset*** of $T$. This is written as $S \subseteq T$ or $T \supseteq S$.

> *Example:*
> $\{-5, 0, 1\}$ is a subset of $\{-5, 0, 1, 4, 10\}$. That is, $\{-5, 0, 1\} \subseteq \{-5, 0, 1, 4, 10\}$.

**D.** The ***union*** of two sets $A$ and $B$ is the set of all elements that are each in $A$ or in $B$ or both. The union is written as $A \cup B$.

> *Example:*
> $\{3, 4\} \cup \{4, 5, 6\} = \{3, 4, 5, 6\}$

**E.** The ***intersection*** of two sets $A$ and $B$ is the set of all elements that are each in **both** $A$ and $B$. The intersection is written as $A \cap B$.

> *Example:*
> $\{3, 4\} \cap \{4, 5, 6\} = \{4\}$

**F.** Two sets sharing no elements are ***disjoint*** or ***mutually exclusive.***

> *Example:*
> $\{-5, 0, 1\}$ and $\{4, 10\}$ are disjoint.

**G.** A ***Venn diagram*** shows how two or more sets are related. Suppose sets $S$ and $T$ aren't disjoint, and neither is a subset of the other. The Venn diagram below shows their intersection $S \cap T$ as a shaded area.

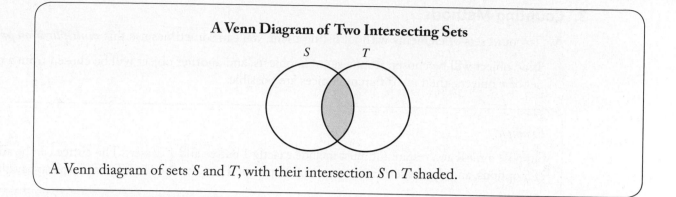

**A Venn Diagram of Two Intersecting Sets**

A Venn diagram of sets $S$ and $T$, with their intersection $S \cap T$ shaded.

**H.** The number of elements in the union of two finite sets $S$ and $T$ is the number of elements in $S$, plus the number of elements in $T$, minus the number of elements in the intersection of $S$ and $T$. That is, $|S \cup T| = |S| + |T| - |S \cap T|$. This is the *general addition rule for two sets.*

*Example:*

$$|\{3, 4\} \cup \{4, 5, 6\}| = |\{3, 4\}| + |\{4, 5, 6\}| - |\{3, 4\} \cap \{4, 5, 6\}| =$$

$$|\{3, 4\}| + |\{4, 5, 6\}| - |\{4\}| = 2 + 3 - 1 = 4.$$

If $S$ and $T$ are disjoint, then $|S \cup T| = |S| + |T|$, since $|S \cap T| = 0$.

**I.** You can often solve word problems involving sets by using Venn diagrams and the general addition rule.

*Example:*

Each of 25 students is taking history, mathematics, or both. If 20 of them are taking history and 18 of them are taking mathematics, how many of them are taking both history and mathematics?

*Solution:* Separate the 25 students into three disjoint sets: the students taking history only, those taking mathematics only, and those taking both history and mathematics. This gives us the Venn diagram below, where $n$ is the number of students taking both courses, $20 - n$ is the number taking history only, and $18 - n$ is the number taking mathematics only.

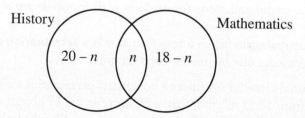

History                                    Mathematics

$20 - n$      $n$      $18 - n$

Since there are 25 students total, $(20 - n) + n + (18 - n) = 25$, so $n = 13$. So, 13 students are taking both history and mathematics. Notice $20 + 18 - 13 = 25$ is an example of the general addition rule for two sets.

## 3. Counting Methods

**A.** To count sets of elements without listing them, you can sometimes use this ***multiplication principle***:

If an object will be chosen from a set of $m$ objects, and another object will be chosen from a different set of $n$ objects, then $mn$ different choices are possible.

> *Example:*
>
> Suppose a meal at a restaurant must include exactly 1 entree and 1 dessert. The entree can be any 1 of 5 options, and the dessert can be any 1 of 3 options. Then $5 \times 3 = 15$ different meals are available.

**B.** Here is a more general version of the multiplication principle: the number of possible choices of 1 object apiece out of any number of sets is the product of the numbers of objects in those sets. For example, when choosing 1 object apiece out of 3 sets with $x$, $y$, and $z$ elements, respectively, $xyz$ different choices are possible. The general multiplication principle also means that when choosing 1 object apiece out of $n$ different sets of exactly $m$ objects apiece, $m^n$ different choices are possible.

> *Example:*
>
> Each time a coin is flipped, the 2 possible results are heads and tails. In a set of 8 consecutive coin flips, think of each flip as a set of those 2 possible results. The 8 flips give us 8 of these 2-element sets. So, the set of 8 flips has a total of $2^8$ possible results.

**C.** A concept often used with the multiplication principle is the ***factorial***. For any integer $n > 1$, $n$ factorial is written as $n!$ and is the product of all the integers from 1 through $n$. Also, by definition, $0! = 1! = 1$.

> *Examples:*
>
> $2! = 2 \times 1 = 2$
>
> $3! = 3 \times 2 \times 1 = 6$
>
> $4! = 4 \times 3 \times 2 \times 1 = 24$, etc.

Two other useful equations for working with factorials are $n! = (n-1)!(n)$ and $(n+1)! = (n!)(n+1)$.

**D.** Any sequential ordering of a set's elements is a ***permutation*** of the set. A permutation is a way to choose elements one by one in a certain order.

The factorial is useful for finding how many permutations a set has. If a set of $n$ objects is being ordered from 1st to $n$th, there are $n$ choices for the 1st object, $n-1$ choices left for the 2nd object, $n-2$ choices left for the 3rd object, and so on, until only 1 choice is left for the $n$th object. So, by the multiplication principle, a set of $n$ objects has $n(n-1)(n-2)\ldots(3)(2)(1) = n!$ permutations.

> *Example:*
>
> The set of letters A, B, and C has $3! = 6$ permutations: ABC, ACB, BAC, BCA, CAB, and CBA.

E. When $0 \leq k \leq n$, each possible choice of $k$ objects out of $n$ objects is a **combination** of $n$ objects taken $k$ at a time. The number of these combinations is written as $\binom{n}{k}$. This is also the number of $k$-element subsets of a set with $n$ elements, since the combinations simply are these subsets. It can be calculated as $\binom{n}{k} = \frac{n!}{k!(n-k)!}$. Note that $\binom{n}{k} = \binom{n}{n-k}$.

---

*Example:*

The 2-element subsets of $S = \{A, B, C, D, E\}$ are the combinations of the 5 letters in $S$ taken 2 at a time. There are $\binom{5}{2} = \frac{5!}{2!3!} = \frac{120}{(2)(6)} = 10$ of these subsets: $\{A, B\}, \{A, C\}, \{A, D\}, \{A, E\}, \{B, C\},$ $\{B, D\}, \{B, E\}, \{C, D\}, \{C, E\},$ and $\{D, E\}$.

For each of its 2–element subsets, a 5-element set also has exactly one 3-element subset containing the elements not in that 2-element subset. For example, in $S$ the 3-element subset $\{C, D, E\}$ contains the elements not in the 2-element subset $\{A, B\}$, the 3-element subset $\{B, D, E\}$ contains the elements not in the 2-element subset $\{A, C\}$, and so on. This shows a 5-element set like $S$ has exactly as many 2-element subsets as 3-element subsets, so $\binom{5}{2} = 10 = \binom{5}{3}$.

---

## 4. Probability

A. Sets and counting methods are also important to **discrete probability**. Discrete probability involves **experiments** with finitely many possible **outcomes**. An **event** is a set of an experiment's possible outcomes.

---

*Example:*

Rolling a 6-sided die with faces numbered 1 to 6 is an experiment with 6 possible outcomes. Let's call these outcomes 1, 2, 3, 4, 5, and 6, each number being the one facing up after the roll. One event in this experiment is that the outcome is 4. This event is written as $\{4\}$.

Another event in the experiment is that the outcome is an odd number. This event has the three outcomes 1, 3, and 5. It is written as $\{1, 3, 5\}$.

---

B. The probability of an event $E$ is written as $P(E)$ and is a number between 0 and 1, inclusive. If $E$ is an empty set of no possible outcomes, then $E$ is **impossible**, and $P(E) = 0$. If $E$ is the set of all possible outcomes of the experiment, then $E$ is **certain**, and $P(E) = 1$. Otherwise, $E$ is possible but uncertain, and $0 < P(E) < 1$. If $F$ is a subset of $E$, then $P(F) \leq P(E)$.

C. If the probabilities of two or more outcomes of an experiment are equal, those outcomes are **equally likely**. For an experiment whose outcomes are all equally likely, the probability of an event $E$ is

$$P(E) = \frac{\text{the number of outcomes in } E}{\text{the total number of possible outcomes}}.$$

---

*Example:*

In the earlier example of a 6-sided die rolled once, suppose the die is fair so that all 6 outcomes are equally likely. Then each outcome's probability is $\frac{1}{6}$. The probability that the outcome is an odd number is $P(\{1, 3, 5\}) = \frac{|\{1, 3, 5\}|}{6} = \frac{3}{6} = \frac{1}{2}$.

---

**D.** Given two events $E$ and $F$ in an experiment, these further events are defined:

(i) "not $E$" is the set of outcomes not in $E$;

(ii) "$E$ or $F$" is the set of outcomes in $E$ or $F$ or both, that is, $E \cup F$;

(iii) "$E$ and $F$" is the set of outcomes in both $E$ and $F$, that is, $E \cup F$.

The probability that $E$ doesn't occur is $P(\text{not } E) = 1 - P(E)$.

The probability that "$E$ or $F$" occurs is $P(E \text{ or } F) = P(E) + P(F) - P(E \text{ and } F)$. This is based on the general addition rule for two sets, given above in section 3.4.2.H.

---

*Example:*

In the example above of a 6-sided die rolled once, let $E$ be the event $\{1, 3, 5\}$ that the outcome is an odd number. Let $F$ be the event $\{2, 3, 5\}$ that the outcome is a prime number. Then

$P(E \text{ and } F) = P(E \cap F) = P(\{3, 5\}) = \dfrac{|\{3, 5\}|}{6} = \dfrac{2}{6} = \dfrac{1}{3}$. So $P(E \text{ or } F) = P(E) + P(F) -$

$P(E \text{ and } F) = \dfrac{3}{6} + \dfrac{3}{6} - \dfrac{2}{6} = \dfrac{4}{6} = \dfrac{2}{3}$.

The event "$E$ or $F$" is $E \cup F = \{1, 2, 3, 5\}$, so $P(E \text{ or } F) = \dfrac{|\{1, 2, 3, 5\}|}{6} = \dfrac{4}{6} = \dfrac{2}{3}$.

---

Events $E$ and $F$ are ***mutually exclusive*** if no outcomes are in $E \cap F$. Then the event "$E$ and $F$" is impossible: $P(E \text{ and } F) = 0$. The special addition rule for the probability of two mutually exclusive events is $P(E \text{ or } F) = P(E) + P(F)$.

**E.** Two events $A$ and $B$ are ***independent*** if neither changes the other's probability. The multiplication rule for independent events $E$ and $F$ is $P(E \text{ and } F) = P(E)P(F)$.

---

*Example:*

In the example above of the 6-sided die rolled once, let $A$ be the event $\{2, 4, 6\}$ and $B$ be the

event $\{5, 6\}$. Then $A$'s probability is $P(A) = \dfrac{|A|}{6} = \dfrac{3}{6} = \dfrac{1}{2}$. The probability of $A$ occurring **if $B$**

**occurs** is $\dfrac{|A \cap B|}{|B|} = \dfrac{|\{6\}|}{|\{5, 6\}|} = \dfrac{1}{2}$, the same as $P(A)$.

Likewise, $B$'s probability is $P(B) = \dfrac{|B|}{6} = \dfrac{2}{6} = \dfrac{1}{3}$. The probability of $B$ occurring **if $A$ occurs**

is $\dfrac{|B \cap A|}{|A|} = \dfrac{\{6\}}{|\{2, 4, 6\}|} = \dfrac{1}{3}$, the same as $P(B)$.

So, neither event changes the other's probability. Thus, $A$ and $B$ are independent. Therefore, by the

multiplication rule for independent events, $P(A \text{ and } B) = P(A)P(B) = \left(\dfrac{1}{2}\right)\left(\dfrac{1}{3}\right) = \dfrac{1}{6}$.

Notice the event "$A$ and $B$" is $A \cap B = \{6\}$, so $P(A \text{ and } B) = P(\{6\}) = \dfrac{1}{6}$.

---

The general addition rule and the multiplication rule discussed above provides that if $E$ and $F$ are independent, $P(E \text{ or } F) = P(E) + P(F) - P(E)P(F)$.

**F.** An event $A$ is **dependent** on an event $B$ if $B$ changes the probability of $A$.

The probability of $A$ occurring if $B$ occurs is written as $P(A|B)$. So, the statement that $A$ is dependent on $B$ can be written as $P(A|B) \neq P(A)$.

A general multiplication rule for any dependent or independent events $A$ and $B$ is $P(A \text{ and } B) = P(A \mid B)P(B)$.

---

*Example:*

In the example of the 6-sided die rolled once, let $A$ be the event $\{4, 6\}$ and $B$ be the event $\{4, 5, 6\}$. Then the probability of $A$ is $P(A) = \dfrac{|A|}{6} = \dfrac{2}{6} = \dfrac{1}{3}$. But the probability that $A$ occurs **if $B$ occurs** is $P(A|B) = \dfrac{|A \cap B|}{|B|} = \dfrac{|\{4, 6\}|}{|\{4, 5, 6\}|} = \dfrac{2}{3}$. Thus, $P(A|B) \neq P(A)$, so $A$ is dependent on $B$.

Likewise, the probability that $B$ occurs is $P(B) = \dfrac{|B|}{6} = \dfrac{3}{6} = \dfrac{1}{2}$. But the probability that $B$ occurs **if $A$ occurs** is $P(B|A) = \dfrac{|B \cap A|}{|A|} = \dfrac{|\{4, 6\}|}{|\{4, 6\}|} = 1$. Thus, $P(B|A) \neq P(B)$, so $B$ is dependent on $A$.

In this example, by the general multiplication rule for events, $P(A \text{ and } B) = P(A|B)P(B) = \left(\dfrac{2}{3}\right)\left(\dfrac{1}{2}\right) = \dfrac{1}{3}$. Likewise, $P(A \text{ and } B) = P(B|A)P(A) = (1)\left(\dfrac{1}{3}\right) = \dfrac{1}{3}$.

Notice the event "$A$ and $B$" is $A \cap B = \{4, 6\} = A$, so $P(A \text{ and } B) = P(\{4, 6\}) = \dfrac{1}{3} = P(A)$.

---

**G.** The rules above can be combined for more complex probability calculations.

---

*Example:*

In an experiment with events $A$, $B$, and $C$, suppose $P(A) = 0.23$, $P(B) - 0.40$, and $P(C) = 0.85$. Also suppose events $A$ and $B$ are mutually exclusive, and events $B$ and $C$ are independent. Since $A$ and $B$ are mutually exclusive, $P(A \text{ or } B) = P(A) + P(B) = 0.23 + 0.40 = 0.63$.

Since $B$ and $C$ are independent, $P(B \text{ or } C) = P(B) + P(C) - P(B)P(C) = 0.40 + 0.85 - (0.40)(0.85) = 0.91$.

$P(A \text{ or } C)$ and $P(A \text{ and } C)$ can't be found from the information given. But we can find that $P(A) + P(C) = 1.08 > 1$. So, $P(A) + P(C)$ can't equal $P(A \text{ or } C)$, which like any probability must be less than or equal to 1. This means that $A$ and $C$ can't be mutually exclusive, and that $P(A \text{ and } C) \geq 0.08$.

Since $A \cap B$ is a subset of $A$, we can also find that $P(A \text{ and } C) \leq P(A) = 0.23$.

And $C$ is a subset of $A \cup C$, so $P(A \text{ or } C) \geq P(C) = 0.85$.

Thus, we've found that $0.85 \leq P(A \text{ or } C) \leq 1$ and that $0.08 \leq P(A \text{ and } C) \leq 0.23$.

---

## 5. Estimation

**A.** Calculating exact answers to complex math questions is often too hard or too slow. Estimating the answers by simplifying the questions may be easier and faster.

One way to estimate is to **round** the numbers in the original question: replace each number with a nearby number that has fewer digits. Often a number is rounded to a nearby multiple of some power of 10.

For any integer $n$ and real number $m$, you can **round $m$ down** to a multiple of $10^n$ by deleting all of $m$'s digits to the right of the digit that stands for multiples of $10^n$.

To **round $m$ up** to a multiple of $10^n$, first add $10^n$ to $m$, then round the result down.

To **round $m$ to the nearest** $10^n$, first find the digit in $m$ that stands for a multiple of $10^{n-1}$. If this digit is 5 or higher, round $m$ up to a multiple of $10^n$. Otherwise, round $m$ down to a multiple of $10^n$.

---

*Examples:*

(i) To round 7651.4 to the nearest hundred (multiple of $10^2$), first notice the digit standing for tens (multiples of $10^1$) is 5.

Since this digit is 5 or higher, round up:

First add 100 to the original number: 7651.4 + 100 = 7751.4.

Then drop all the digits to the right of the one standing for multiples of 100 to get 7700.

Notice that 7700 is closer to 7651.4 than 7600 is, so 7700 is the nearest 100.

(ii) To round 0.43248 to the nearest thousandth (multiple of $10^{-3}$), first notice the digit standing for ten-thousandths (multiples of $10^{-4}$) is 4. Since 4 < 5, round down: just drop all the digits to the right of the digit standing for thousandths to get 0.432.

---

**B.** Rounding can simplify complex arithmetical calculations and give rough answers. If you keep more digits of the original numbers, the answers are usually more exact, but the calculations take longer.

---

*Example:*

You can roughly estimate the value of $\dfrac{(298.534 + 58.296)}{1.4822 + 0.937 + 0.014679}$ by rounding the numbers in the dividend to the nearest 10 and the numbers in the divisor to the nearest 0.1:

$$\frac{(298.534 + 58.296)}{1.4822 + 0.937 + 0.014679} \approx \frac{300 + 60}{1.5 + 0.9 + 0} = \frac{360}{2.4} = 150$$

---

**C.** Sometimes it is easier to estimate by rounding to a multiple of a number other than 10, like the nearest square or cube of an integer.

*Examples:*

(i) You can roughly estimate the value of $\dfrac{2447.16}{11.9}$ by noting first that both the dividend and the divisor are near multiples of 12: 2448 and 12. So $\dfrac{2447.16}{11.9} \approx \dfrac{2448}{12} = 204$.

(ii) You can roughly estimate the value of $\sqrt{\dfrac{8.96}{24.82 \times 4.057}}$ by noting first that each decimal number in the expression is near the square of an integer: $8.96 \approx 9 = 3^2$, $24.82 \approx 25 = 5^2$, and $4.057 \approx 4 = 2^2$. So $\sqrt{\dfrac{8.96}{24.82 \times 4.057}} \approx \sqrt{\dfrac{3^2}{5^2 \times 2^2}} = \sqrt{\dfrac{3^2}{10^2}} = \dfrac{3}{10}$.

**D.** Sometimes finding a **range** of possible values for an expression is more useful than finding a single estimated value. The range's **upper bound** is the smallest number found to be greater than (or greater than or equal to) the expression's value. The range's **lower bound** is the largest number found to be less than (or less than or equal to) the expression's value.

*Example:*

In the equation $x = \dfrac{2.32^2 - 2.536}{2.68^2 + 2.79}$, each decimal is greater than 2 and less than 3. So, $\dfrac{2^2 - 3}{3^2 + 3} < x < \dfrac{3^2 - 2}{2^2 + 2}$. Simplifying these fractions, we find that $x$ is in the range $\dfrac{1}{12} < x < \dfrac{7}{6}$. The range's lower bound is $\dfrac{1}{12}$, and the upper bound is $\dfrac{7}{6}$.

## 6. Sequences and Series

**A.** A **sequence** is an algebraic function whose domain includes only positive integers. A function $a(n)$ that is a sequence can be written as $a_n$. The domain of an **infinite sequence** is the set of all positive integers. For any positive integer $n$, the domain of a **finite sequence of length** $n$ is the set of the first $n$ positive integers.

*Example:*

(i) The function $a(n) = n^2 + \left(\dfrac{n}{5}\right)$ is an infinite sequence $a_n$ whose domain is the set of all positive integers $n = 1, 2, 3, \ldots$. Its value at $n = 3$ is $a_3 = 3^2 + \dfrac{3}{5} = 9.6$.

(ii) The same function $a(n) = n^2 + \left(\dfrac{n}{5}\right)$ restricted to the domain $\{1, 2, 3\}$ is a finite sequence of length 3 whose range is $\{1.2, 4.4, 9.6\}$.

(iii) An infinite sequence like $b_n = (-1)^n(n!)$ can be written out by listing its values in the order $b_1, b_2, b_3, \ldots, b_n, \ldots$: that is, $-1, 2, -6, \ldots, (-1)^n(n!), \ldots$

The value $(-1)^n(n!)$ is the $n^{\text{th}}$ term of the sequence.

**B.** A *series* is the sum of a sequence's terms.

For an infinite sequence $a(n)$, the **infinite series** $\sum\limits_{n=1}^{\infty} a(n)$ is the sum of the sequence's infinitely many terms, $a_1 + a_2 + a_3 + \dots$

The sum of the first $k$ terms of sequence $a_n$ is called a **partial sum**. It is written as $\sum\limits_{i=1}^{k} a_i$, or $a_1 + \dots + a_k$.

---

*Example:*

The infinite series based on the function $a(n) = n^2 + \left(\dfrac{n}{5}\right)$ is $\sum\limits_{i=1}^{\infty} n^2 + \left(\dfrac{n}{5}\right)$. It's the sum of the infinitely many terms $\left(1^2 + \dfrac{1}{5}\right) + \left(2^2 + \dfrac{2}{5}\right) + \left(3^2 + \dfrac{3}{5}\right) + \dots$

The partial sum of the first three terms of the same function $a(n) = n^2 + \left(\dfrac{n}{5}\right)$ is

$$\sum_{i=1}^{3} a_i = \left(1^2 + \dfrac{1}{5}\right) + \left(2^2 + \dfrac{2}{5}\right) + \left(3^2 + \dfrac{3}{5}\right) = 1.2 + 4.4 + 9.6 = 15.2.$$

---

# 3.5   Reference Sheets

# Arithmetic and Decimals

## ABSOLUTE VALUE:

$|x|$ is $x$ if $x \geq 0$ and $-x$ if $x < 0$.

For any $x$ and $y$, $|x + y| \leq |x| + |y|$.

$\sqrt{x^2} = |x|$.

## EVEN AND ODD NUMBERS:

| | |
|---|---|
| Even × Even = Even | Even × Odd = Even |
| Odd × Odd = Odd | Even + Even = Even |
| Even + Odd = Odd | Odd + Odd = Even |

## ADDITION AND SUBTRACTION:

$x + 0 = x = x - 0$

$x - x = 0$

$x + y = y + x$

$x - y = -(y - x) = -y + x$

$(x + y) + z = x + (y + z)$

If $x$ and $y$ are both positive, then $x + y$ is also positive.

If $x$ and $y$ are both negative, then $x + y$ is negative.

## DECIMALS:

Add or subtract decimals by lining up their decimal points:

| | |
|---|---|
| $\phantom{+}17.6512$ | $\phantom{-}653.2700$ |
| $+653.2700$ | $-17.6512$ |
| $670.9212$ | $635.6188$ |

To multiply decimal $A$ by decimal $B$:

First, ignore the decimal points, and multiply $A$ and $B$ as if they were integers.

Next, if decimal $A$ has $n$ digits to the right of its decimal point, and decimal $B$ has $m$ digits to the right of its decimal point, place the decimal point in $A \times B$ so it has $m + n$ digits to its right.

To divide decimal $A$ by decimal $B$, first move the decimal points of $A$ and $B$ equally many digits to the right until $B$ is an integer, then divide as you would integers.

## QUOTIENTS AND REMAINDERS:

The quotient $q$ and the remainder $r$ of dividing positive integer $x$ by positive integer $y$ are unique positive integers such that

$y = xq + r$ and $0 \leq r < x$.

The remainder $r$ is 0 if and only if $y$ is divisible by $x$. Then $x$ is a factor of $y$.

## MULTIPLICATION AND DIVISION:

$x \times 1 = x = \dfrac{x}{1}$

$x \times 0 = 0$

If $x \neq 0$, then $\dfrac{x}{x} = 1$.

$\dfrac{x}{0}$ is undefined.

$xy = yx$

If $x \neq 0$ and $y \neq 0$, then $\dfrac{x}{y} = \dfrac{1}{\left(\dfrac{y}{x}\right)}$.

$(xy)z = x(yz)$

$xy + xz = x(y + z)$

If $y \neq 0$, then $\left(\dfrac{x}{y}\right) + \left(\dfrac{z}{y}\right) = \dfrac{(x + z)}{y}$

If $x$ and $y$ are both positive, then $xy$ is also positive.

If $x$ and $y$ are both negative, then $xy$ is positive.

If $x$ is positive and $y$ is negative, then $xy$ is negative.

If $xy = 0$, then $x = 0$ or $y = 0$, or both.

## SCIENTIFIC NOTATION:

To convert a number in scientific notation $A \times 10^n$ into regular decimal notation, move $A$'s decimal point $n$ places to the right if $n$ is positive, or $|n|$ places to the left if $n$ is negative.

To convert a decimal to scientific notation, move the decimal point $n$ spaces so that exactly one nonzero digit is to its left. Multiply the result by $10^n$ if you moved the decimal point to the left or by $10^{-n}$ if you moved it to the right.

# Exponents

## SQUARES, CUBES, AND SQUARE ROOTS:

Every positive number has two real square roots, one positive and the other negative. The table below shows the positive square roots rounded to the nearest hundredth.

| $n$ | $n^2$ | $n^3$ | $\sqrt{n}$ |
|-----|-------|-------|-----------|
| 1 | 1 | 1 | 1 |
| 2 | 4 | 8 | 1.41 |
| 3 | 9 | 27 | 1.73 |
| 4 | 16 | 64 | 2 |
| 5 | 25 | 125 | 2.24 |
| 6 | 36 | 216 | 2.45 |
| 7 | 49 | 343 | 2.65 |
| 8 | 64 | 512 | 2.83 |
| 9 | 81 | 729 | 3 |
| 10 | 100 | 1,000 | 3.16 |

## EXPONENTIATION:

| Formula | Example |
|---------|---------|
| $x^1 = x$ | $2^1 = 2$ |
| $x^0 = 1$ | $2^0 = 1$ |
| If $x \neq 0$, then $x^{-1} = \frac{1}{x}$. | $2^{-1} = \frac{1}{2}$ |
| If $x > 1$ and $y > 1$, then $x^y > x$. | $2^3 = 8 > 2$ |
| If $0 < x < 1$ and $y > 1$, then $x^y < x$. | $0.2^3 = 0.008 < 0.2$ |
| $(x^y)^z = x^{yz} = (x^z)^y$ | $(2^3)^4 = 2^{12} = (2^4)^3$ |
| $x^{y+z} = x^y x^z$ | $2^7 = 2^3 2^4$ |
| If $x \neq 0$, then $x^{y-z} = \frac{x^y}{x^z}$. | $2^{5-3} = \frac{2^5}{2^3}$ |
| $(xz)^y = x^y z^y$ | $6^4 = 2^4 3^4$ |
| If $z \neq 0$, then $\left(\frac{x}{z}\right)^y = \frac{x^y}{z^y}$ | $\left(\frac{3}{4}\right)^2 = \frac{3^2}{4^2} = \frac{9}{16}$ |
| If $z \neq 0$, then $x^{\frac{y}{z}} = (x^y)^{\frac{1}{z}} = (x^{\frac{1}{z}})^y$. | $4^{\frac{2}{3}} = (4^2)^{\frac{1}{3}} = (4^{\frac{1}{3}})^2$ |

# Algebraic Expressions and Linear Equations

## TRANSLATING WORDS INTO MATH OPERATIONS:

| $x + y$ | $x - y$ | $xy$ | $\dfrac{x}{y}$ | $x^y$ |
|---|---|---|---|---|
| *x added to y*<br>*x increased by y*<br>*x more than y*<br>*x plus y*<br>*the sum of x and y*<br>*the total of x and y* | *x decreased by y*<br>*difference of x and y*<br>*y fewer than x*<br>*y less than x*<br>*x minus y*<br>*x reduced by y*<br>*y subtracted from x* | *x multiplied by y*<br>*the product of x and y*<br>*x times y* | *x divided by y*<br>*x over y*<br>*the quotient of x and y*<br>*the ratio of x to y* | *x to the power of y*<br>*x to the $y^{th}$ power* |
| | | **If $y = 2$:**<br>*double x*<br>*twice x* | **If $y = 2$:**<br>*half of x*<br>*x halved* | **If $y = 2$:**<br>*x squared* |
| | | **If $y = 3$:**<br>*triple x* | | **If $y = 3$:**<br>*x cubed* |

## MANIPULATING ALGEBRAIC EXPRESSIONS:

| Technique | Example |
|---|---|
| Factor to combine like terms | $3xy - 9y = 3y(x - 3)$ |
| Divide out common factors | $\dfrac{(3xy - 9y)}{(x - 3)} = \dfrac{3y(x - 3)}{(x - 3)} = 3y(1) = 3y$ |
| Multiply two expressions by multiplying each term of one expression by each term of the other | $(3x - 4)(9y + x) = 3x(9y + x) - 4(9y + x)$<br>$\qquad\qquad = 3x(9y) + 3x(x) + -4(9y) + -4(x)$<br>$\qquad\qquad = 27xy + 3x^2 - 36y - 4x$ |
| Substitute constants for variables | If $x = 3$ and $y = -2$, then $3xy - x^2 + y$ can be evaluated as $3(3)(-2) - (3)^2 + (-2) = -18 - 9 - 2 = -29$. |

**SOLVING LINEAR EQUATIONS:**

| Technique | Example |
|---|---|
| Isolate a variable on one side of an equation by doing the same operations on both sides of the equation. | Solve the equation $\frac{(5x-6)}{3} = 4$ like this:<br>(1) Multiply both sides by 3 to get $5x - 6 = 12$.<br>(2) Add 6 to both sides to get $5x = 18$.<br>(3) Divide both sides by 5 to get $x = \frac{18}{5}$. |
| To solve two equations with two variables $x$ and $y$:<br>(1) Express $x$ in terms of $y$ using one of the equations.<br>(2) Substitute that expression for $x$ to make the second equation have only the variable $y$.<br>(3) Solve the second equation for $y$.<br>(4) Substitute the solution for $y$ into the first equation to solve for $x$. | Solve the equations A: $x - y = 2$ and B: $3x + 2y = 11$:<br>(1) From A, $x = 2 + y$.<br>(2) In B, substitute $2 + y$ for $x$ to get $3(2 + y) + 2y = 11$.<br>(3) Solve B for $y$: $6 + 3y + 2y = 11$<br>$\qquad 6 + 5y = 11$<br>$\qquad\quad 5y = 5$<br>$\qquad\quad\ y = 1$.<br>(4) Since $y = 1$, from A we find $x = 2 + 1 = 3$. |
| Alternative technique:<br>(1) Multiply both sides of one equation or both equations so that the coefficients on $y$ have the same absolute value in both equations.<br>(2) Add or subtract the two equations to remove $y$ and solve for $x$.<br>(3) Substitute the solution for $x$ into the first equation to find the value of $y$. | Solve the equations A: $x - y = 2$ and B: $3x + 2y = 11$:<br>(1) Multiply both sides of A by 2 to get $2x - 2y = 4$.<br>(2) Add the equation in (1) to equation B:<br>$\qquad 2x - 2y + 3x + 2y = 4 + 11$<br>$\qquad\qquad 5x = 15$<br>$\qquad\qquad\ x = 3$.<br>(3) Since $x = 3$, from A we find $3 - y = 2$, so $y = 1$. |

# Factoring, Quadratic Equations, and Inequalities

## SOLVING EQUATIONS BY FACTORING:

| Techniques | Example |
|---|---|
| (1) Start with a polynomial equation.<br>(2) Add or subtract expressions until 0 is on one side of the equation.<br>(3) Write the nonzero side as a product of factors.<br>(4) Set each factor to 0 to find a simple equation giving a solution to the original equation. | $x^3 - 2x^2 + x = -5(x-1)^2$<br>$x^3 - 2x^2 + x + 5(x-1)^2 = 0$<br>(i) $x(x^2 - 2x + 1) + 5(x-1)^2 = 0$<br>(ii) $x(x-1)^2 + 5(x-1)^2 = 0$<br>(iii) $(x+5)(x-1)^2 = 0$<br>$x + 5 = 0$ or $x - 1 = 0$. So, $x = -5$ or $x = 1$. |

## FORMULAS FOR FACTORING:

$a^2 - b^2 = (a-b)(a+b)$

$a^2 + 2ab + b^2 = (a+b)(a+b)$

$a^2 - 2ab + b^2 = (a-b)(a-b)$

## THE QUADRATIC FORMULA:

For any quadratic equation $ax^2 + bx + c = 0$ with $a \neq 0$, the roots are

$$x = \frac{-b + \sqrt{b^2 - 4ac}}{2a} \text{ and } x = \frac{-b - \sqrt{b^2 - 4ac}}{2a}$$

These roots are two distinct real numbers unless $b^2 - 4ac \leq 0$.

If $b^2 - 4ac = 0$, the equation has only one root: $\frac{-b}{2a}$.

If $b^2 - 4ac < 0$, the equation has no real roots.

## SOLVING INEQUALITIES:

| Explanation | Example |
|---|---|
| As in solving an equation, the same number can be added to or subtracted from both sides of the inequality, or both sides can be multiplied or divided by a positive number, without changing the order of the inequality. But multiplying or dividing an inequality by a negative number reverses the order of the inequality.<br><br>Thus, $6 > 2$, but $(-1)(6) < (-1)(2)$. | To solve the inequality $\frac{(5x-1)}{-2} < 3$ for $x$, isolate $x$:<br>(1) $5x - 1 > -6$ (multiplying both sides by $-2$, reversing the order of the inequality)<br>(2) $5x > -5$    (add 1 to both sides)<br>(3) $x > -1$    (divide both sides by 5) |

## LINES IN THE COORDINATE PLANE:

An equation $y = mx + b$ defines a line with slope $m$ whose $y$–intercept is $b$.

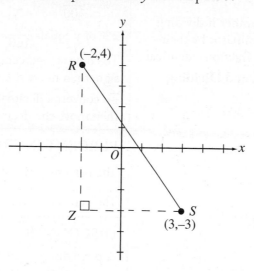

For a line through two points $(x_1, y_1)$ and $(x_2, y_2)$ with $x_1 \neq x_2$, the slope is $m = \dfrac{(y_2 - y_1)}{(x_2 - x_1)}$. Given the known point $(x_1, y_1)$ and the slope $m$, any other point $(x, y)$ on the line satisfies the equation $m = \dfrac{(y - y_1)}{(x - x_1)}$.

Above, the line's slope is $\dfrac{(-3 - 4)}{(3 - (-2))} = \dfrac{7}{5}$. To find an equation of the line, we can use the point $(3, -3)$:

$$y - (-3) = \left(-\frac{7}{5}\right)(x - 3)$$

$$y + 3 = \left(-\frac{7}{5}\right)x + \frac{21}{5}$$

$$y = \left(-\frac{7}{5}\right)x + \frac{6}{5}$$

So, the $y$–intercept is $\dfrac{6}{5}$.

Find the $x$–intercept like this:

$$0 = \left(-\frac{7}{5}\right)x + \frac{6}{5}$$

$$\left(\frac{7}{5}\right)x = \frac{6}{5}$$

$$x = \frac{6}{7}$$

The graph shows both these intercepts.

# Rates, Ratios, and Percents

## FRACTIONS:

### Equivalent or Equal Fractions:

Two fractions stand for the same number if dividing each fraction's numerator and denominator by their greatest common divisor makes the fractions identical.

### Adding, Subtracting, Multiplying, and Dividing Fractions:

$$\frac{a}{b} + \frac{c}{d} = \frac{ad}{bd} + \frac{bc}{bd}; \frac{a}{b} - \frac{c}{d} = \frac{ad}{bd} - \frac{bc}{bd}$$

$$\frac{a}{b} \times \frac{c}{d} = \frac{ac}{bd}; \frac{a}{b} \div \frac{c}{d} = \frac{ad}{bc}$$

## MIXED NUMBERS:

A mixed number of the form $a\frac{b}{c}$ equals the fraction $\frac{ac + b}{c}$.

## RATE:

distance = rate × time

## PROFIT:

Gross profit = Revenues − Expenses, or

Gross profit = Selling price − Cost.

## INTEREST:

Simple annual interest =

(principal) × (interest rate) × (time)

Compound interest over $n$ periods =

(principal) × (1 + interest per period)$^n$ − principal

## PERCENTS:

$x\% = \frac{x}{100}$.

$x\%$ of $y$ equals $\frac{xy}{100}$.

To convert a percent to a decimal, drop the percent sign, then move the decimal point two digits left.

To convert a decimal to a percent, add a percent sign, then move the decimal point two digits right.

## PERCENT INCREASE OR DECREASE:

The percent increase from $x$ to $y$ is $100\left(\frac{y - x}{x}\right)\%$.

The percent decrease from $x$ to $y$ is $100\left(\frac{x - y}{x}\right)\%$.

## DISCOUNTS:

A price discounted by $n$ percent becomes $(100 − n)$ percent of the original price.

A price discounted by $n$ percent and then by $m$ percent becomes $(100 − n)(100 − m)$ percent of the original price.

## WORK:

$\frac{1}{r} + \frac{1}{s} = \frac{1}{h}$, where $r$ is how long one individual takes to do an amount of work, $s$ is how long a second individual takes to do that much work, and $h$ is how long they take to do that much work when both are working at the same time.

## MIXTURES:

| | Number of units of a substance or mixture | Amount of an ingredient per unit of the substance or mixture | Total amount of that ingredient in the substance or mixture |
|---|---|---|---|
| Substance A | X | M | X × M |
| Substance B | Y | N | Y × N |
| Mixture of A and B | X + Y | $\frac{(X \times M) + (Y \times N)}{X + Y}$ | (X × M) + (Y × N) |

# Statistics, Sets, and Counting Methods

**STATISTICS:**

| Concept | Definition for a set of $n$ numbers ordered from least to greatest | Example with data set $\{4, 4, 5, 7, 10\}$ |
|---|---|---|
| **Mean** | The sum of the $n$ numbers, divided by $n$ | $\dfrac{(4 + 4 + 5 + 7 + 10)}{5} = \dfrac{30}{5} = 6$ |
| **Median** | The middle number if $n$ is odd; The mean of the two middle numbers if $n$ is even. | 5 is the middle number in $\{4, 4, 5, 7, 10\}$. |
| **Mode** | The number that appears most often in the set | 4 is the only number that appears more than once in $\{4, 4, 5, 7, 10\}$. |
| **Range** | The largest number in the set minus the smallest | $10 - 4 = 6$ |
| **Standard Deviation** | Calculate like this: (1) Find the arithmetic mean, (2) Find the differences between each of the $n$ numbers and the mean, (3) Square each of the differences, (4) Find the average of the squared differences, and (5) Take the nonnegative square root of this average. | (1) The mean is 6. (2) $-2, -2, -1, 1, 4$ (3) $4, 4, 1, 1, 16$ (4) $\dfrac{26}{5} = 5.2$ (5) $\sqrt{5.2}$ |

**SETS:**

| Concept | Notation for finite sets $S$ and $T$ | Example |
|---|---|---|
| **Number of elements** | $|S|$ | $S = \{-5, 0, 1\}$ is a set with $|S| = 3$. |
| **Subset** | $S \subseteq T$ ($S$ is a subset of $T$); $S \supseteq T$ ($T$ is a subset of $S$) | $\{-5, 0, 1\}$ is a subset of $\{-5, 0, 1, 4, 10\}$. |
| **Union** | $S \cup T$ | $\{3, 4\} \cup \{4, 5, 6\} = \{3, 4, 5, 6\}$ |
| **Intersection** | $S \cap T$ | $\{3, 4\} \cap \{4, 5, 6\} = \{4\}$ |
| **The general addition rule for two sets** | $|S \cup T| = |S| + |T| - |S \cap T|$ | $|\{3, 4\} \cup \{4, 5, 6\}| = $ $|\{3, 4\}| + |\{4, 5, 6\}| - |\{3, 4\} \cap \{4, 5, 6\}| = $ $|\{3, 4\}| + |\{4, 5, 6\}| - |\{4\}| = 2 + 3 - 1 = 4.$ |

**COUNTING METHODS:**

| Concept and Equations | Examples |
|---|---|
| **Multiplication Principle:** <br> The number of possible choices of 1 element apiece from the sets $A_1, A_2, \ldots, A_n$ is $|A_1| \times |A_2| \times \ldots \times |A_n|$. | The number of possible choices of 1 element apiece from the sets $S = \{-5, 0, 1\}$, $T = \{3, 4\}$, and $U = \{3, 4, 5, 6\}$ is $|S| \times |T| \times |U| = 3 \times 2 \times 4 = 24$. |
| **Factorial:** <br> $n! = n \times (n - 1) \times \ldots \times 1$ <br> $0! = 1! = 1$ <br> $n! = (n - 1)!(n)$ | $4! = 4 \times 3 \times 2 \times 1 = 24$ <br> $4! = 3! \times 4$ |
| **Permutations:** <br> A set of $n$ objects has $n!$ permutations | The set of letters A, B, and C has $3! = 6$ permutations: ABC, ACB, BAC, BCA, CAB, and CBA. |
| **Combinations:** <br> The number of possible choices of $k$ objects from a set of $n$ objects is $\binom{n}{k} = \dfrac{n!}{k!(n-k)!}$. | The number of 2-element subsets of set $\{A, B, C, D, E\}$ is $$\binom{5}{2} = \frac{5!}{2!3!} = \frac{120}{(2)(6)} = 10.$$ The 10 subsets are: $\{A, B\}, \{A, C\}, \{A, D\}, \{A, E\}, \{B, C\}, \{B, D\}, \{B, E\}, \{C, D\}, \{C, E\}$, and $\{D, E\}$. |

# Probability, Sequences, and Partial Sums

## PROBABILITY:

| Concept | Definition, Notation, and Equations | Example: Rolling a die with 6 numbered sides once |
|---|---|---|
| **Event** | A set of outcomes of an experiment | The event of the outcome being an odd number is the set $\{1, 3, 5\}$. |
| **Probability** | The probability $P(E)$ of an event $E$ is a number between 0 and 1, inclusive. If each outcome is equally likely, $P(E) =$ $\dfrac{\text{(the number of possible outcomes in E)}}{\text{(the total number of possible outcomes)}}$. | If the 6 outcomes are equally likely, the probability of each outcome is $\frac{1}{6}$. The probability that the outcome is an odd number is $P(\{1, 3, 5\}) =$ $\dfrac{|\{1, 3, 5\}|}{6} = \dfrac{3}{6} = \dfrac{1}{2}$. |
| **Conditional Probability** | The probability that $E$ occurs if $F$ occurs is $P(E|F) = \dfrac{|E \cap F|}{|F|}$. | $P(\{1, 3, 5\}|\{1, 2\}) = \dfrac{|\{1\}|}{|\{1, 2\}|} = \dfrac{1}{2}$ |
| **Not $E$** | The set of outcomes not in event $E$: $P(\text{not } E) = 1 - P(E)$. | $P(\text{not}\{3\}) = \dfrac{6-1}{6} = \dfrac{5}{6}$ |
| **$E$ and $F$** | The set of outcomes in both $E$ and $F$, that is, $E \cap F$; $P(E \text{ and } F) = P(E \cap F) = P(E|F)P(F)$. | For $E = \{1, 3, 5\}$ and $F = \{2, 3, 5\}$: $P(E \text{ and } F) = P(E \cap F) = P(\{3, 5\}) =$ $\dfrac{|\{3, 5\}|}{6} = \dfrac{2}{6} = \dfrac{1}{3}$ |
| **$E$ or $F$** | The set of outcomes in $E$ or $F$ or both, that is, $E \cup F$; $P(E \text{ or } F) = P(E) + P(F) - P(E \text{ and } F)$. | For $E = \{1, 3, 5\}$ and $F = \{2, 3, 5\}$: $P(E \text{ or } F) = P(E) + P(F) - P(E \text{ and } F)$ $= \dfrac{3}{6} + \dfrac{3}{6} - \dfrac{2}{6} = \dfrac{4}{6} = \dfrac{2}{3}$. |
| **Dependent and Independent Events** | $E$ is dependent on $F$ if $P(E|F) \neq P(E)$. $E$ and $F$ are independent if neither is dependent on the other. If $E$ and $F$ are independent, $P(E \text{ and } F) = P(E)P(F)$. | For $E = \{2, 4, 6\}$ and $F = \{5, 6\}$: $P(E|F) = P(E) = \dfrac{1}{2}$, and $P(F|E) = P(F) = \dfrac{1}{3}$, so $E$ and $F$ are independent. Thus $P(E \text{ and } F) = P(E)P(F) = \left(\dfrac{1}{2}\right)\left(\dfrac{1}{3}\right) = \dfrac{1}{6}$. |

## SEQUENCE:

An algebraic function whose domain contains only positive integers.

**Example:** Function $a(n) = n^2 + \left(\dfrac{n}{5}\right)$ with the domain of all positive integers $n = 1, 2, 3, \dots$ is an infinite sequence $a_n$.

## PARTIAL SUM:

The sum $\displaystyle\sum_{i=1}^{k} a_i$ of the first $k$ terms of series $a_n$ is a partial sum of the series.

**Example:** For the function $a(n) = n^2 + \left(\dfrac{n}{5}\right)$, the partial sum of the first three terms is

$$\sum_{i=1}^{3} a_i = \left(1^2 + \dfrac{1}{5}\right) + \left(2^2 + \dfrac{2}{5}\right) + \left(3^2 + \dfrac{3}{5}\right).$$

**To register for the GMAT™ exam, go to www.mba.com/register**

**4.0   Data Insights Review**

# 4.0 Data Insights Review

To prepare for the Data Insights section of the GMAT™ and succeed in graduate business programs, you need basic skills in analyzing data. This chapter is about the kinds of data shown in tables and charts. It's only a brief overview, so if you find unfamiliar terms, consult outside resources to learn more. Before reading this chapter, you may want to read this guidebook's Section 3.4.1, "Statistics," and Section 7.2.2, "Generalizations and Predictions," in the *GMAT™ Official Guide 2023–2024* book to review basic statistics and inductive generalization. to review basic statistics and inductive generalization.

Section 4.1, "Data Sets and Types," includes these topics:

1. Data Sets
2. Qualitative Data
3. Quantitative Data

Section 4.2, "Data Displays," includes these topics:

1. Tables
2. Qualitative Charts
3. Quantitative Charts

Section 4.3, "Data Patterns" includes these topics:

1. Distributions
2. Trends and Correlations

# 4.1 Data Sets and Types

## 1. Data Sets

A. A ***data set*** is an organized collection of data about a specific topic. A data set can be shown with one or more tables, charts, or both.

> *Example:*
>
> One data set might have data about all the employees in a company's human resources division, such as their first names, last names, home addresses, phone numbers, positions, salaries, hiring dates, and full-time or part-time statuses.

B. A ***case*** is an individual or thing about which data is collected. Often the same types of data about many cases together form a data set. Then a table or chart can show those types of data for all the cases.

> *Example:*
>
> In the example above, each employee in the human resources department is a case.

C. A ***variable*** is any specific type of data collected about a set of cases. For each case in a data set, the variable has a ***value***.

> *Example:*
>
> In the example above, each type of data collected about the employees is a variable: *first name* is one variable, *home address* is another variable, *phone number* is a third variable, and so on. If Zara is an employee in the human resources department, one value of the variable *first name* is "Zara."

In a simple table, the top row often names the variables. Each column shows one variable's values for all the cases. In a chart, labels usually say which variables are shown.

D. The value of a **dependent variable** depends on the values of one or more other variables in the data set. An **independent variable** is not dependent.

> *Example:*
>
> In a data set of revenues, expenses, and profits, *revenue* and *expense* are independent variables. But *profit* is a dependent variable because profit is calculated as revenue minus expense. For each case, the value of the variable *profit* depends on the values of the variable's *revenue* and *expense*.

E. A **data point** gives the value of a specific variable in a specific case. A cell in a table usually stands for a data point.

> *Example:*
>
> In the example above, one data point might be that Zara's position is assistant manager. That is, the data point gives the value "assistant manager" for the variable *position* in Zara's case.

F. A **record** is a list of the data points for one case. A row in a table usually shows one record. In a chart, a record might be shown as a point, a line, a bar, or a small shape with a specific position or length.

> *Example:*
>
> In the example above, one record might list Zara's first name, last name, home address, phone number, position, salary, hiring date, and full-time or part-time status.

## 2. Qualitative Data

A. **Qualitative data** is any type of data that doesn't use numbers to stand for a quantity. Statements, words, names, letters, symbols, algebraic expressions, colors, images, sounds, computer files, and web links are all qualitative data. Even data that looks numeric is qualitative if the numbers don't stand for quantities.

> *Example:*
>
> Phone numbers are qualitative data. That's because they don't stand for quantities and aren't used in math—for example, they are generally not summed, multiplied, or averaged.

B. **Nominal data** is any type of qualitative data that's not ordered in any relevant way. The statistical measures of mean, median, and range don't apply to nominal data because those measures need an ordering that nominal data lacks. But even in a set of nominal data, some values may appear more often than others. So, the statistical measure of mode does apply to nominal data because the mode is simply the value that appears most often. To review these statistical terms, refer to Section 3.4.1, "Statistics."

> *Example:*
>
> In the example above, the first names of the human resource department's employees are nominal data if their alphabetical order doesn't matter in the data set. Suppose three of the employees share the first name "Amy," but no more than two of the employees share any other first name. Then "Amy" is the mode of the first names of the department's employees because it's the first name that appears most often in the data set.

C. ***Ordinal data*** is qualitative data ordered in a way that matters in the data set. Because ordinal data is qualitative, its values can't be added, subtracted, multiplied, or divided. So, the statistical measures of mean and range do not apply to ordinal data because they're calculated with those arithmetic operations. However, the statistical measure of median does apply to ordinal data because finding a median only requires putting the values in an order. The statistical measure of mode also applies, just as it does for nominal data.

> *Example:*
>
> In a data set for a weekly schedule of appointments, the weekdays Monday, Tuesday, Wednesday, Thursday, and Friday are ordinal data. These days are in an order that matters to the schedule, but they're not numbers and don't measure quantities. Suppose the data set lists seven appointments: two on Monday, two on Tuesday, and three on Thursday. The fourth appointment is the median in the schedule because three appointments are before it and three are after it. The fourth appointment is on Tuesday, so "Tuesday" is the median value of the variable *weekday* for the appointments in this data set. "Thursday" is the mode because more of the appointments are on Thursday than on any other day.

D. ***Binary data*** takes only two values, like "true" and "false." Binary data is ordinal if the order of the two values matters, but nominal otherwise. Tables may show binary values with two words like "yes" and "no," or with two letters like "T" and "F," or simply with a check mark or "X" standing for one of the two values, and a blank space standing for the other.

> *Example:*
>
> In the example above of the data set of employees in a human resource department, their employment status is a binary variable with two values: "full time" and "part time." A table might show the employment status data in a column simply titled "Full Time," with a checkmark for each full-time employee and a blank for each part-time employee.

E. ***Partly ordered data*** has an order among some cases but not among others. The statistical measure of median does not apply to a set of partly ordered values, though it might apply to a subset whose values are all fully ordered.

*Example:*

Suppose a family tree shows how people over several generations were related as parents, children, and siblings, but doesn't show when each person was born. This tree lets us partly order the family members by the variable *age*. For example, suppose the family tree shows that Haruto's children were Honoka and Akari and Honoka's child was Minato. Since we know that all parents are older than their children, we can tell that Haruto was older than Honoka and Akari, and that Honoka was older than Minato. That also means Haruto was older than Minato. But we cannot determine whether Akari is older or younger than her sister Honoka. We can't even deduce with certainty whether Akari is older or younger than her nephew Minato. So, the family tree only partly orders the family members by age.

## 3. Quantitative Data

**A.** *Quantitative data* is data about quantities measured in numbers. Quantitative values can be added, multiplied, averaged, and so on. The statistical measures of mean, median, mode, range, and standard deviation all apply to quantitative data.

*Example:*

In the example above of the data set of the employees in the human resource department, the salaries are quantitative data. They're amounts of money shown as numbers.

**B.** Quantitative data is *continuous* if it measures something that can be infinitely divided.

*Examples:*

Temperatures are continuous data. That's because for any two different temperatures, some third temperature is between them—warmer than one and cooler than the other. Likewise, altitudes are continuous data. For any two different altitudes, some third altitude is higher than one and lower than the other.

A set of continuous quantitative values rarely has a mode. Because infinitely many of these values are possible, usually no two of them in a data set are exactly alike.

**C.** Quantitative data that isn't continuous is *discrete*.

*Examples:*

The numbers of students taking different university courses are discrete data because they're whole numbers. A course normally can't have a fractional number of students.

As another example, prices in a currency are discrete data because they can't be divided beyond the currency's smallest denomination. Suppose one price in euros is €3.00, and another is €3.01. No price in euros is larger than the first and smaller than the second because the currency has no denomination below one euro cent (1/100 of a euro). That means you can't have a price of €3.005, for example. The prices in euros aren't continuous, so they're discrete.

Counted numbers of people, objects, or events are generally discrete data.

**D.** *Interval data* uses a measurement scale whose number zero doesn't stand for a complete absence of the factor measured. So, for interval data, a measurement above zero doesn't show how much greater than nothing the measured quantity is. Because of this, the ratio of two measurements in interval data isn't the ratio of the two measured quantities.

*Examples:*

Dates given in years are interval data. In different societies' calendars, the year "0" stands for different years. The year 0 in the Gregorian calendar was roughly the year 3760 in the Hebrew calendar, −641 in the Islamic calendar, and −78 in the Indian National calendar. In none of these calendars does 0 stand for the very first year ever. This means, for example, that the ratio of the numbers in the two years 500 CE and 1500 CE in the Gregorian calendar isn't the ratio of two amounts: the year 500 CE isn't 1/3 the amount of the year 1500 CE.

As another example, temperatures given in degrees Celsius, or Fahrenheit are also interval data. The temperature 0 degrees Celsius is 32 degrees Fahrenheit. In neither temperature scale does 0 degrees mean absolute 0, the complete absence of heat. This means, for example, that the ratio of the numbers in the temperatures 30°F and 60°F isn't the ratio of two amounts of heat. Thus, 60°F isn't twice as hot as 30°F.

In a measurement scale for interval data, each unit stands for the same amount. That is, any two measurements that differ by the same number of units stand for two quantities that differ by the same amount.

*Examples:*

In the example above of dates given in years, the year 1500 CE was 1000 years after 500 CE, because 1500 − 500 = 1000. Likewise, the year 1600 CE was 1000 years after 600 CE, because 1600 − 600 = 1000. Although you can't divide one year by another to find a real ratio, you can subtract one year from another to find a real-time interval—in this case, 1000 years.

Likewise, 60°F is the same amount warmer than 40°F as it is cooler than 80°F. A 20°F difference in two measured temperatures always stands for the same real difference in heat between those temperatures.

**E.** *Ratio data* uses a measurement scale whose number zero stands for the absence of the measured factor. In ratio data, as in interval data, the difference between two measurements stands for the actual difference between the measured amounts. However, in ratio data, unlike interval data, the ratio of two measurements also stands for the actual ratio of the measured amounts.

*Examples:*

Measured weights are ratio data, whether they're in kilograms or pounds. That's because 0 kilograms stands for a complete absence of weight, as does 0 pounds. So, the ratio of 10 kilograms to 5 kilograms is a ratio of two real weights. Because the ratio of 10 to 5 is 2 to 1, 10 kilograms is twice as heavy as 5 kilograms, and 10 pounds is twice as heavy as 5 pounds.

As another example, temperatures measured in degrees Kelvin are ratio data. That's because 0°K stands for absolute zero, the complete absence of heat. Thus, 200°K is really twice as hot as 100°K. As explained above, this isn't the case with temperatures measured in degrees Celsius or Fahrenheit, which are interval data.

F.  **Logarithmic data** use a measurement scale whose higher values stand for amounts exponentially farther apart. For logarithmic data, as for ratio data, the number zero stands for a complete absence. But in logarithmic data, the higher two measurements a certain number of units apart are, the greater the real difference between the measured amounts is.

> *Example:*
>
> Noise measured in decibels is logarithmic data. Although 0 decibels indicates complete silence, a noise of 30 decibels is 10 times as loud as a noise of 20 decibels, not just 1.5 times as loud. And the real difference in loudness between 40 decibels and 30 decibels is 10 times the real difference in loudness between 30 decibels and 20 decibels, even though the first difference and the second difference are each 10 decibels.

Because the units at higher levels on a logarithmic scale stand for greater amounts of difference, you can't just sum and divide logarithmic data to find a statistical mean. Nor can you subtract one logarithmic measurement from another to find a statistical range. Finding the mean and range require more complex calculations, which you won't have to do on the GMAT.

## 4.2 Data Displays

### 1. Tables

A.  A **table** shows data in rows and columns. In a simple table, the top row shows the names of the variables and is called the **header**. Below the header, usually each row shows one record, each column shows one variable, and each cell shows one data point. Sometimes another row above the header has the table's title or description. Sometimes a column or a few rows within the table are used only to group the records by category. Likewise, a row or a few columns within the table are sometimes used only to group the variables by category. Sometimes a row or column shows totals, averages, or other operations on the values in other rows or columns.

*Example:*

The table below shows revenues, expenses, and profits for two branches of Village Shoppe for one year. The top row is the header listing the independent variables *revenue* and *expense* and the dependent variable *profit*. In each row, the profit is just the revenue minus the expense.

The table has only four rows of records. These are the third row showing the Mapleton branch's January-June finances, the fourth row showing the Mapleton branch's April-December finances, the sixth row showing the Elmville branch's January-June finances, and the seventh row showing the Elmville branch's April-December finances. The second row "Mapleton branch" serves to group the third and fourth rows together. Likewise, the fifth row "Elmville branch" serves to group the sixth and seventh rows together. The bottom row "Annual grand totals" doesn't show a record, but rather sums the values in the four records for each of the three variables.

| Village Shoppe | Revenue | Expense | Profit |
|---|---|---|---|
| Mapleton branch | | | |
| January-June | 125000 | 40000 | 85000 |
| April-December | 90000 | 35000 | 55000 |
| Elmville branch | | | |
| January-June | 85000 | 30000 | 55000 |
| April-December | 115000 | 25000 | 90000 |
| **Annual grand totals** | **415000** | **130000** | **285000** |

**B.** Sometimes a table's title or description explains the data shown. To understand the data, always study any title or description.

*Example:*

In the table below, the title says the populations are in **thousands**. So, to find the total population aged 44 and under, add 63,376 thousand and 86,738 thousand. This gives 150,114 thousand, which is 150,114,000. If you only read the numbers without noticing the title, you'll get the wrong result for the total population aged 44 and under.

| Population by Age Group (in thousands) | |
|---|---|
| Age | Population |
| 17 years and under | 63,376 |
| 18–44 years | 86,738 |
| 45–64 years | 43,845 |
| 65 years and over | 24,051 |

## 2. Qualitative Charts

**A.** Many different types of charts show qualitative data. This book's Section 3.4.2, "Sets," discusses one type of qualitative chart, the ***Venn diagram***. Here we describe a few other common types. But the GMAT may also challenge you with unfamiliar types of charts this book doesn't discuss. To understand any type of chart, study its labels. The labels will tell you how to read the chart's various points, lines, shapes, symbols, and colors. Several labels may be together, sometimes inside a rectangle on the chart, to make a ***legend***.

**B.** A *network diagram* has lines connecting small circles or other shapes. Each small shape is a *node* standing for an individual, and each line stands for a relationship between two individuals. In some network diagrams, the lines are one-way or two-way arrows standing for one-way or two-way relationships.

*Example:*

In the network diagram below, the lettered nodes stand for six pen pals: Alice, Ben, Cathy, Dave, Ellen, and Frank. The arrows show who got a letter from whom in the past month. Each arrow points from the pen pal who sent the letter to the one who got it. A two-way arrow means both the pen pals got letters from each other. This diagram tells us many facts about the pen pals and their relationships over the past month. For example, it shows who got the most letters (Cathy received three) and who got the fewest (Frank received none).

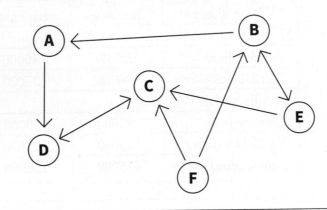

**C.** A *tree diagram* is a type of network diagram that shows partly ordered data like organizational structures, ancestral relationships, or conditional probabilities. In a tree diagram, each relationship is one way.

*Example:*

Expanding on the example in 4.1.2.E above, the tree diagram below shows how all of Haruto's descendants are related. Each line connects a parent above to his or her child below. The diagram shows how Haruto has two children, four grandchildren, and one great-grandchild. From the diagram we can tell that Akari is older than her grandchild Mei, and that Himari and Minato are cousins. However, we can't tell whether Akari, Mei, or Himari is older than Minato.

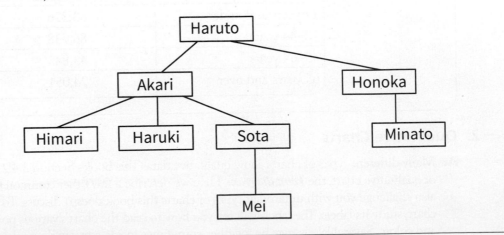

**D.** In a *flowchart*, each node stands for a step in a process. Arrows direct you from each step to the next. An arrow pointing back to an earlier step tells you to repeat that step. A flowchart usually has at least three types of nodes. *Process nodes* stand for actions to take and are usually rectangles. *Decision nodes* show questions to answer and are usually diamond shaped. At least two labeled arrows lead from each decision node to show how choosing the next step depends on how you answer the question. *Terminal nodes* show the start or end of the process and are usually oval.

*Example:*

The flowchart below shows a simple process for getting cereal from a store. The top oval shows the first step, going to the store. The arrow below it then takes us to a process node saying to look for a cereal we like. For the third step, we reach a decision node asking us whether we found the cereal we wanted. If we did, we follow the node's "Yes" arrow to another process node telling us to buy the cereal we found, then move on to the bottom terminal node telling us to go home. Otherwise, we follow the node's "No" arrow to a second decision node asking whether the store offers other good cereal choices. If it doesn't, we follow another "No" arrow telling us to give up and go home. But if the store does offer other good cereal choices, we follow a "Yes" arrow taking us back to the "look for a cereal you like" step to peruse the choices again. We repeat the loop until we either find a cereal we want to buy or decide the store has no more good cereal choices. Since the store won't have infinitely many cereals to consider, we eventually end at the bottom terminal node and go home.

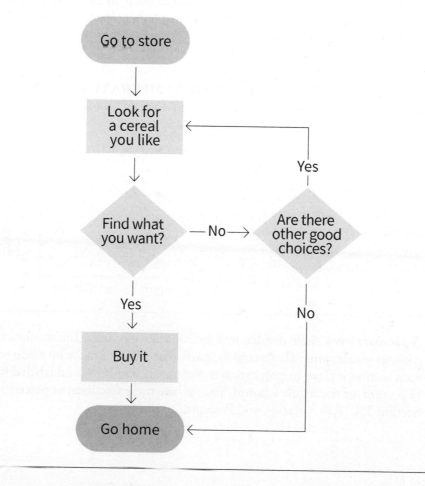

## 3. Quantitative charts

**A.** Here we discuss a few common types of charts that normally show quantitative data. The GMAT may also use rarer types this book doesn't discuss. To understand any type of quantitative chart, study the description and any labels to find out what cases and variables are shown, and how. Also notice any axes, these show the measurement scales used. Some quantitative charts have no axes, while others have one, two, or, rarely, three or more. For each axis, notice whether it shows 0 and any negative values, or whether it starts above 0. Study the numbers on the axes and note any named units the numbers stand for. You must read the axes correctly to read the data shown.

*Example:*

In the chart below, labels say the scale on the left is for the temperature data, and the scale on the right is for the precipitation data. The bottom axis shows four months of the year, spaced three months apart. The chart's title tells us each data point gives the **average** temperature or precipitation in City X during a given month. This implies that the temperatures and precipitations shown are averages over many years. Suppose we're asked to find the average temperature and precipitation in City X in April. To do this, we don't have to calculate averages of any of the values shown. Those values are **already** averages. So, to find the average temperature for April, we simply read the April temperature data point by noting it's slightly lower than the 15 on the temperature scale at the left. Likewise, to find the average precipitation for April, we read the April precipitation data point by noticing it's about as high as the 8 on the precipitation scale on the right. This means the chart says that in April, the average temperature is about 14° Celsius and the average precipitation about 8 centimeters. Since the question is only about April, the data shown for January, July, and October are irrelevant.

### AVERAGE TEMPERATURE AND PRECIPITATION IN CITY X

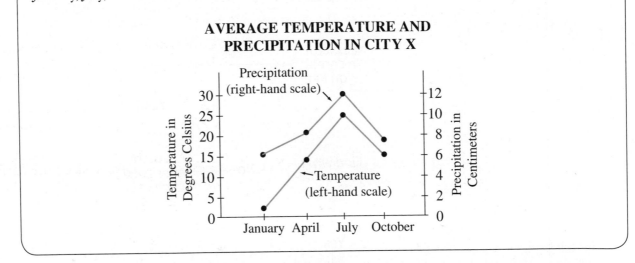

**B.** A *pie chart* has a circle divided into sections like pie slices. The sections make up the whole circle without overlapping. They stand for parts that together make up some whole amount. Usually, each section is sized in proportion to the part it stands for, and labeled with that part's fraction, or percent, of the whole amount. You can use these fractions, or percents, in calculations. Refer to Section 3.3, "Rates, Ratios, and Percents," to review how.

*Example:*

In the pie chart below, the sections are sized in proportion to their percent amounts. These percents add up to 100%. Suppose we're told that Al's weekly net salary is $350 and asked how many of the categories shown each individually took at least $80 of that $350. To answer, first we find that $\frac{\$80}{\$350}$ is about 23%, which means $80 or more of Al's salary went to a category, if and only if, at least 23% went to that category. So, the graph shows exactly two categories that each took at least $80 of Al's salary: the category *Savings* took 25% of his salary and *Rent and Utilities* took 30%.

**DISTRIBUTION OF AL'S WEEKLY NET SALARY**

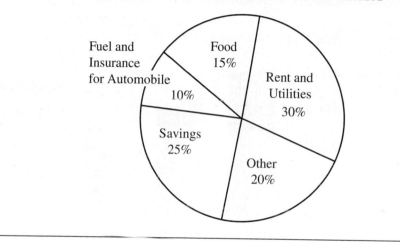

C. A *bar chart* has a series of vertical or horizontal bars standing for a set of cases. A simple bar chart has only one quantitative variable. The bars' different heights or lengths show that variable's values for different cases.

A *grouped* bar chart may have more than one quantitative variable. Its bars are grouped together. Each group either shows the values of different variables for one case, or else the values of related cases for one variable.

And in a *stacked* bar chart, segments are stacked into bars. Each segment inside a bar stands for part of an amount, and the whole bar stands for the whole amount.

*Example:*

The bar chart below is both grouped and stacked. Each pair of grouped bars shows population figures for one of three towns. In each pair, the bar on the left shows the town's population in 2010, and the bar on the right shows the town's population in 2020. Inside each bar, the lower segment shows how many people in the town were under age 30, and the upper segment shows how many were age 30 or older. For example, the chart's fifth bar shows that in 2010 Ceburg's population was around 2,000, including about 1,100 people under 30 and 900 people 30 or older. And the chart's sixth bar shows that by 2020, Ceburg's population had grown to around 2,400, including about 1,200 people under 30 and 1,200 people 30 or older. By reading the chart this way to find the amounts shown, we can also estimate various other amounts, like the three towns' combined total number of residents 30 or older in 2020.

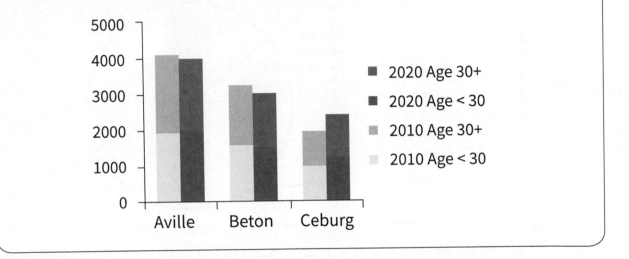

**D.** A ***histogram*** looks like a vertical bar chart but works differently. In a histogram, each bar stands for a range of values that the same quantitative variable can take. These ranges don't overlap. Together they usually include every value the variable can take, or at least every value it does take in some population. The bars are in order left to right, from the one standing for the lowest range of values to the one standing for the highest range. Each bar's height shows the number or proportion of times the variable's value is in the range the bar stands for. A bar chart makes it easy to see how the values are distributed.

*Example:*

The histogram below shows the measured weights of 31 gerbils. Each bar's height shows how many gerbils were in a specific weight range. For example, the bar farthest left says 3 gerbils each weighed from 60 to 65 grams. The histogram doesn't show any individual gerbil's weight. However, it does give us some statistical information. For example, by adding the numbers of gerbils in the different weight ranges, we can tell that the 16th-heaviest of the 31 gerbils weighed between 75 and 80 grams. This means the gerbils' median weight was in that range. The histogram also shows that the gerbils mainly weighed between 70 and 85 grams apiece, though several weighed less or more.

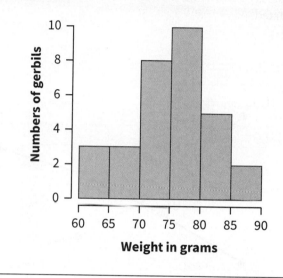

E. A *line chart* often shows how the values of one or more quantitative variables change over time. Typically, the horizontal axis has the time scale, and the vertical axis has one or more scales for the variable or variables. One or more lines connect the data points. Different lines may stand either for different variables or for a single variable applied to different cases. Line charts make it easy to see trends and correlations.

Some line charts show probability distributions instead of changes over time, as we'll see in section 4.3.1 below.

*Examples:*

In section 4.2.3.A above, the chart of average monthly temperatures and precipitations is a line chart whose two variables have two separate scales, one on the left and one on the right.

The line chart below shows how many toasters of each of three different brands were sold each year from 2017 to 2022. Each sloping line shows how sales changed for one of the three brands during that period. The legend on the bottom says which line stands for which toaster brand. All three lines use the scale on the left, whose numbers stand for thousands of units sold annually. The chart shows that over the six years, annual sales of Crispo toasters increased dramatically, while annual sales of Brownita toasters declined to almost zero, and annual sales of Toastador toasters fluctuated.

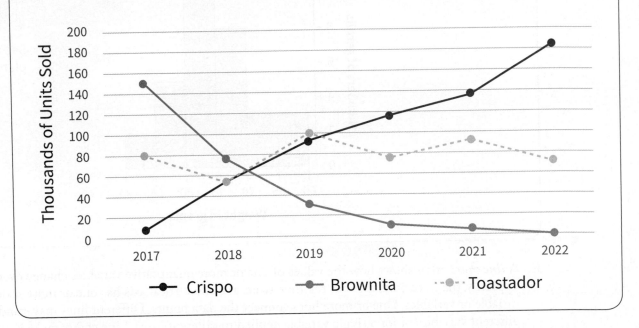

**F.** A *scatterplot* has at least two quantitative variables, one on each axis. For each case in the data, a dot's position shows the variables' values. No lines connect the scattered dots, but a straight or curved line through the scatterplot may show an overall trend in the data. Sometimes the dots have a few different shapes or colors to show they stand for cases in different categories. And in scatterplots called *bubble charts*, the dots have different sizes standing for values of a third variable.

Scatterplots are useful for showing correlations. They also show how much individual cases fit an overall correlation or deviate from it.

*Example:*

The scatterplot below shows measured widths and lengths of leaves on two plants. Each dot stands for one leaf. The dot's position stands for the leaf's width and length in centimeters, as the scatterplot's two axes show. The legend says how one set of dots stand for leaves on the first plant, and another set for leaves on the second. The scatterplot shows that in general, the longer leaves tend to be wider, and vice versa. It also shows how leaves on the second plant tend to be somewhat longer and wider than those on the first, with some exceptions.

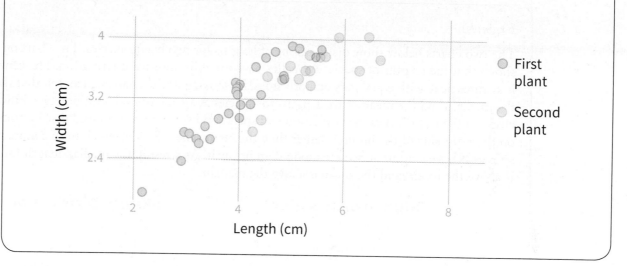

# 4.3 Data Patterns

## 1. Distributions

**A.** A data ***distribution*** is a pattern in how often different values appear in data. How data in a sample is distributed can tell you how likely different values are to appear in the same population outside the sample. In the *GMAT™ Official Guide 2023–2024* book, Section 7.2.2, "Generalizations and Predictions," discusses generalizations and predictions based on samples.

**B.** A distribution is ***uniform*** when each value occurs more or less equally often. It's less uniform when the differences between how frequently the values occur are greater. The more uniform a distribution is for a sample, the better it supports the conclusion that the distribution for other cases in the population is likewise uniform.

*Example:*

Suppose the six faces on a die are numbered 1 to 6. And suppose that when rolled sixty times, the die comes up 1 eleven times, 2 nine times, 3 ten times, 4 eleven times, 5 ten times, and 6 nine times. This isn't a **perfectly** uniform distribution, because the six values 1 to 6 didn't occur exactly ten times apiece. However, because each value did occur between nine and eleven times, the distribution is **fairly** uniform. This suggests that each of the six values is about equally likely to occur again when the die is rolled, and that the distribution of the values for future rolls will stay fairly uniform.

C. A variable's values are often distributed unevenly. Sometimes one central value occurs most often, with other values occurring less often the farther they are from the central value. When this type of distribution is *normal*, each value below the central value occurs just as often as the value equally far above the central value. For a perfectly normal distribution, the central value is the mean, the median, and the mode. When plotted on a chart, a normal distribution is bell shaped, with a central hump tapering off equally into tails on both sides. But a distribution with a larger tail on one side of the hump than the other is not normal but *skewed*. For a skewed distribution, the mean is often farther out on the larger tail than the median is.

---

*Example:*

The two charts below show distributions of lengths for two beetle species. The chart on the left shows that the lengths of species A beetles have roughly a normal distribution. The central hump is symmetrical, with equal tails on both sides. By looking at the chart, we can tell that the mode, the median, and the mean of the lengths for species A are all around 5 millimeters. However, the chart on the right shows that the lengths of species B beetles have a skewed distribution. The tail on the right side of the hump is larger than the tail on the left side, which means more beetles of species B have lengths above the mode than below it. As a result, the median length for species B is above the mode, and the mean is above the median.

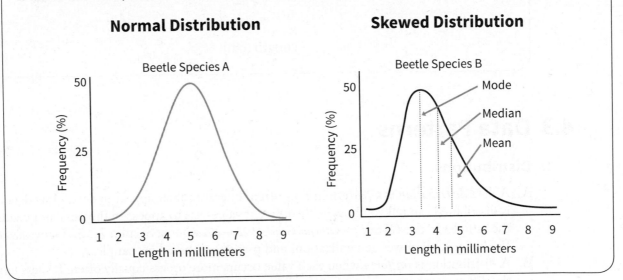

---

D. The more tightly clustered a distribution is around a central value, the higher and narrower the hump is, and the smaller the tails are. A more tightly clustered distribution also has a smaller standard deviation, as discussed in Section 3.4.1, "Statistics." The more tightly clustered a distribution is for an observed sample, the more likely a new case from the population outside that sample is to have a value near the distribution's central value.

*Example:*

For each of three tasks, the chart below shows how frequently it takes workers different lengths of time in minutes to complete that task. Even though the bottom axis shows times from 1 to 5 minutes, it doesn't stand for a single period starting at 1 minute and ending at 5 minutes. Instead, it stands for a range of lengths of task completion times.

Notice how the chart uses smooth curves to show the frequencies of different completion times. That suggests it shows trends idealized from the observed data points, which could be shown more precisely as separate dots or bars.

For each task, the distribution of completion times is uniform, with a mode, median, and mean of 3 minutes. But the completion times are most tightly clustered around 3 minutes for Task A, and least tightly clustered for Task C. That means the standard deviation of the completion times is lowest for Task A and highest for Task C. It also means the probability is higher that an individual worker will take close to 3 minutes to complete Task A than to complete Task C. A worker's completion time for Task C is less predictable and likely to be farther from 3 minutes. So, the chart gives **stronger evidence** for the conclusion that finishing Task A will take a worker between 2 and 4 minutes than for the conclusion that finishing Task C will take that worker between 2 and 4 minutes.

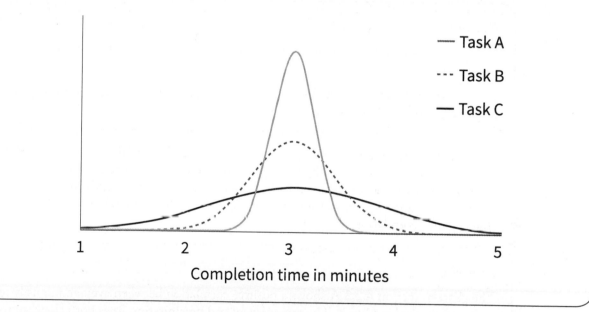

— Task A

--- Task B

— Task C

Completion time in minutes

E. Data distributions take many other shapes too. Some have two or more humps, and others have random variations in frequency among adjacent values. In general, the less the values in a sample cluster around one central hump, the larger the standard deviation is, and the less predictable the values are for cases in the population outside the observed sample.

## 2. Trends and Correlations

A. Charts often show trends over time. They may show that a variable's values increase, decrease, fluctuate, or change in cycles. They may also show values of different plotted variables changing the same ways or opposite ways.

Other things equal, an observed trend over a period is evidence that the same trend extends at least slightly before and after that period. This evidence is stronger the longer the observed trend has lasted and the more varied the conditions it's lasted through. Generalizing from a longer observed period with more varied conditions is like generalizing from a larger sample, as discussed in Section 7.2.2,

"Generalizations and Predictions" of the *GMAT™ Official Guide 2023–2024* book. But the odds increase of other factors disrupting the observed trend at times more distant from the observed period, and in situations whose conditions differ more from those observed.

---

*Example:*

The line chart in section 4.2.3.E above shows that annual sales of Crispo toasters rose from fewer than 10,000 in 2017 to over 180,000 in 2022. If this trend continues another year, even more than 180,000 Crispo toasters will be sold in 2023. However, many factors might disrupt Crispo's surging popularity. For example, another company might start making better or cheaper toasters, drawing consumers away from Crispo toasters. Or broader social, economic, or technological changes might reduce demand for toasters altogether. The more years pass outside the observed period of 2017 through 2022, the more likely such disruptions become. So, the observed trend gives stronger evidence that annual Crispo toaster sales will be over 180,000 in 2023 than it gives that they'll still be over 180,000 in 2050.

---

**B.** Two quantitative or ordinal variables are ***positively correlated*** if they both tend to be higher in the same cases. They're ***negatively correlated*** if one tends to be higher in cases where the other is lower.

---

*Examples:*

If warmer days tend to be rainier in a certain region, then temperature and precipitation are positively correlated there.

But if warmer days tend to be drier in a different region, then temperature and precipitation are negatively correlated in that second region.

---

**C.** On a line chart, the lines standing for positively correlated variables tend to slope up or down together. The more consistently the slopes match, the stronger the positive correlation. But when two variables are negatively correlated, the line standing for one tends to slope up where the other slopes down, and vice versa. The more consistently the lines slope in opposite directions, the stronger the negative correlation.

---

*Examples:*

The chart in section 4.2.3.A shows a positive correlation between average monthly temperature and precipitation in City X. The temperature and precipitation lines both slope up together from January through July, and then slope down together.

The chart in section 4.2.3.E shows a negative correlation between annual sales of Crispo toasters and annual sales of Brownita toasters. Throughout this chart, the line standing for Crispo toaster sales slopes up and the line standing for Brownita toaster sales slopes down. However, the chart shows no clear positive or negative correlation of Crispo or Brownita toaster sales with Toastador toaster sales. The line standing for Toastador toaster sales fluctuates, sometimes sloping up and sometimes down. It shows no consistent trend relative to the other two lines. So, the chart doesn't clearly support a prediction that in future years Toastador sales will increase or decrease as Crispo or Brownita sales do the same or the opposite.

---

**D.** When a scatterplot shows a positive correlation, the dots tend to cluster around a line that slopes up. When it shows a negative correlation, they tend to cluster around a line that slopes down. The stronger the correlation, the more tightly the dots cluster around the sloped line. If the dots spread farther away from the sloped line, or cluster around a line with a less consistent slope, the correlation is weaker or non-existent.

*Example:*

The scatterplot in section 4.2.3.F shows leaf width as positively correlated with leaf length for both plants. The dots mostly cluster around a line sloping up, which means wider leaves tend to be longer and vice versa. Thus, the scatterplot supports a prediction that if another leaf on one of the plants is measured, it too will probably be wider if it's longer. However, the correlation in the scatterplot isn't perfect. For example, the dot farthest to the right is lower than each of about a dozen dots to its left. That dot farthest to the right stands for a leaf that's both longer and thinner than any of the leaves those other dozen dots stand for. This inconsistency in the correlation somewhat weakens the scatterplot's support for the prediction that another leaf measured on one of the plants will be wider if it's longer.

**E.** Values of a nominal variable may also be associated with higher or lower values of an ordinal or quantitative variable. Different values of two nominal variables can also be associated with each other.

*Examples:*

Species is a nominal variable. Individuals of some species tend to weigh more than individuals of other species, so different values of the nominal variable species are associated with higher or lower values of the quantitative variable weight.

As another example, university students majoring in certain subjects like physics are more likely to take certain courses like statistics than university students majoring in other subjects like theater are, even though university major and enrollment in a course are both nominal variables.

An association involving a nominal variable like species isn't a positive or negative correlation because nominal variables aren't ordered; one species isn't greater or less than another. Still, these nominal associations can be shown in qualitative charts and tables and can support predictions. Knowing an animal's species gives you some evidence about roughly how much it will likely weigh and knowing a university student's major gives you some evidence about what courses they're most likely to take.

**To register for the GMAT™ exam go to** www.mba.com/register

# 5.0 Data Insights

# 5.0 Data Insights

This chapter describes the Data Insights section of the GMAT™ exam, explains what it measures, discusses the five types of Data Insights questions, and offers strategies for answering them.

Because most Data Insights questions are interactive, you must use a computer to access them fully. Among Data Insights questions, only the Data Sufficiency questions can be fully shown on paper. So, those are the only Data Insights practice questions in this book.

> **For additional Data Insights practice questions, go to** mba.com/my-account **and access the Online Question Bank using the code from the inside front cover.**

## Overview of the Data Insights Section

The Data Insights section measures your skill at analyzing data shown in formats often used in real business situations. You'll need this skill to make informed decisions as a future business leader. Data Insights questions ask you to assess multiple sources and types of information—graphic, numeric, and verbal—as they relate to one another.

This section asks you to:

- Use math, verbal reasoning, and data analysis,

- Solve connected problems together, and

- Give answers in different formats, not just traditional multiple choice.

Many Data Insights questions ask you to study graphs and sort tables to find information. These questions don't require advanced statistics or spreadsheet expertise. Other Data Insights questions ask you to tell whether given data is enough to solve a math problem, but don't ask you to solve it. You may also use an approved calculator.

You have 45 minutes to answer the 20 questions in the Data Insights section, an average of two minutes, fifteen seconds per question. Throughout the section are questions of five types. Some need multiple responses. A question may use math, data analysis, verbal reasoning, or all three. Questions involving math require knowing the topics reviewed in Chapter 3, "Math Review": Value order, Factors, Algebra, Equalities, Inequalities, Rates, Ratios, Percents, Statistics, Sets, Counting, Probability, Estimation, and Series. Questions involving data analysis require understanding different types of data shown in tables or graphs, finding patterns in that data, and using other skills reviewed in Chapter 4, "Data Insights Review." Questions involving verbal reasoning require understanding texts, reasoning, evaluating arguments, and using other skills reviewed in Chapter 7, "Verbal Review" of the *GMAT™ Official Guide 2023–2024* book.

To prepare for the Data Insights section, first review basic math, data analysis, and verbal reasoning skills to make sure you know enough to answer the questions. Then practice on GMAT questions from past exams.

## Special Features:

- Unlike the other sections of the GMAT exam, the Data Insights section sometimes shows two or more questions on a single screen. When it does, you can change your answers before clicking "Next" to go on to the next screen. But once you're on a new screen, you can't return to the previous screen.

- The Data Insights section uses some math, but it doesn't ask you to calculate by hand. An onscreen calculator with basic functions is available for this section. For more information, please go to **mba.com/exampolicies**.

# 5.1 What Is Measured

The Data Insights section measures how well you use data to solve problems. Specifically, it tests the skills described below:

| Skill Category | Details | Examples |
|---|---|---|
| **Apply** | Understand principles, rules, or other concepts. Use them in a new context or predict what would follow if new information were added. | • Tell whether new examples follow or break given rules<br>• Tell how new situations would affect a trend<br>• Use given principles to draw conclusions about new data |
| **Evaluate** | Judge the quality of given information | • Tell whether information from one source supports or weakens a claim in another source<br>• Tell whether given information is enough to justify a course of action<br>• Judge how well evidence supports an argument or plan<br>• Find errors or gaps in given information |
| **Infer** | Draw unstated conclusions from given information | • Calculate an outcome's probability using given data<br>• Tell whether statements follow logically from the information given<br>• Say what a term means in a given context<br>• Find a rate of change in data gathered over time |
| **Recognize** | Identify information given explicitly, including specific facts, details, or relationships between pieces of information | • Find agreements and disagreements between information sources<br>• Find how strongly two variables are correlated<br>• Give a ranking based on a table by combining categories (for example, saying which product maximizes revenue and minimizes costs)<br>• Tell which data is given as evidence in an argument |
| **Strategize** | Find ways to work toward a goal given specific needs or constraints | • Choose a plan that minimizes risks and maximizes value<br>• Identify trade-offs needed to reach a goal<br>• Tell which math formula gives the desired result<br>• Decide which ways of completing a task meet given needs |

# 5.2 Question Types and Test-Taking Strategies

The Data Insights section has five types of questions: Multi-Source Reasoning, Table Analysis, Graphics Interpretation, Two-Part Analysis, and Data Sufficiency. We describe each below.

## 1. Multi-Source Reasoning

**What you see:**

- Two or three tabs on the left side of your screen. Each tab shows a written passage, a table, a graph, or another form of information. The different tabs may show information in different forms. You click on the tabs to see what's on them and find what you need to answer the questions.

**Example of information sources presented on multiple tabs:**

| Techniques | Artifacts | Budget |
|---|---|---|

For outside laboratory tests, the museum's first-year budget for the Kaxna collection allows unlimited IRMS testing, and a total of $7,000—equal to the cost of 4 TL tests plus 15 radiocarbon tests, or the cost of 40 ICP-MS tests—for all other tests. For each technique applied by an outside lab, the museum is charged a fixed price per artifact.

- A question with answer choices on the right side of your screen. With each set of tabs, three questions appear one at a time.

**The response type:**

- Some questions are traditional multiple choice, with five answer choices

- Others are "conditional statement" questions. This means that each question gives a condition. Below that are three rows with contents such as sentences, phrases, words, numbers, or formulas. For each row, mark "yes" or "true" if the row's contents meet the given condition, and "no" or "false" otherwise.

  - Mark one answer PER ROW.

  - You must mark all three rows correctly to get credit for the question.

**Example of a conditional statement question:**

For each of the following artifacts in the museum's Kaxna collection, select *Yes* if, based on the museum's assumptions, a range of dates for the object's creation can be obtained using one of the techniques in the manner described. Otherwise, select *No*.

Yes  No

○  ○  Bronze statue of a deer

○  ○  Fired-clay pot

○  ○  Wooden statue of a warrior

## Tips for Answering Multi-Source Reasoning Questions

- **Answer using only the information given.**

  The tabs show all the information you need to answer correctly. If you already know about the topic, don't use that knowledge to answer. Use only the information in the tabs.

- **Analyze each source of information.**

  As you read a text passage, note each statement's role. Refer to Section 7.1, "Analyzing Passages," of the *GMAT™ Official Guide 2023–2024* book for explanation.

Notice labels and scales to understand the data shown in tables and graphs. Refer to Chapter 4, "Data Insights Review," for explanation.

- **Read the whole question.**

  You need to understand what each question is asking you to do. For example, some questions ask you to spot conflicts between the information sources. Others ask you to draw conclusions by combining information from different sources. There are also questions that ask you to judge which information sources are relevant to a question.

  While answering the questions, you can always click on the tabs to review any of the information.

## 2. Table Analysis

**What you see:**

- A data table like a spreadsheet. You can sort it by each data column.

Example of data table with sorting drop-down menu:

The table displays data on *Brazilian agricultural* products in 2009.

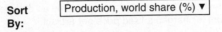

Sort By: Production, world share (%) ▼

| Commodity | Production, world share (%) | Production, world rank | Exports, world share (%) | Exports, world rank |
|---|---|---|---|---|
| Pork | 4 | 4 | 12 | 4 |
| Cotton | 5 | 5 | 10 | 4 |
| Corn | 8 | 4 | 10 | 2 |
| Chickens | 15 | 3 | 38 | 1 |
| Beef | 16 | 2 | 22 | 1 |
| Sugar | 21 | 1 | 44 | 1 |
| Soybeans | 27 | 2 | 40 | 2 |
| Coffee | 40 | 1 | 32 | 1 |
| Orange juice | 56 | 1 | 82 | 1 |

**The response type:**

- The questions are in "conditional statement" form. Each question gives a condition. Below that are three rows with contents such as sentences, phrases, words, numbers, or formulas. For each row, mark "yes" or "true" if the row's contents meet the condition, and "no" or "false" otherwise.

- Mark one answer PER ROW.

- You must mark all three rows correctly to get credit for the question.

Example of a conditional statement question:

For each of the following statements, select *Yes* if the statement can be shown to be true based on the information in the table. Otherwise select *No*.

| Yes | No | |
|---|---|---|
| ○ | ○ | No individual country produces more than one-fourth of the world's sugar. |
| ○ | ○ | If Brazil produces less than 20% of the world's supply of any commodity listed in the table, Brazil is not the world's top exporter of that commodity. |
| ○ | ○ | Of the commodities in the table for which Brazil ranks first in world exports, Brazil produces more than 20% of the world's supply. |

## Tips for Answering Table Analysis Questions

- **Study the table and any text around it to learn what kind of data it shows.**

  Knowing what kind of data is in the table helps you find the information you need.

- **Study the condition in the question.**

  The question gives a condition like "*is consistent with the information provided*" or "*can be inferred from the information provided*." Understanding that condition helps you understand how to mark each row.

- **Read each answer row to decide how to sort the table.**

  Often an answer row's contents hint at how to sort the table by one or more columns to make the data you need easier to find.

- **Judge whether each answer row's contents meet the given condition.**

  In each row, you can only mark one of the two answer choices, and only one is right. Think about whether the row's contents meet the condition in the question.

## 3. Graphics Interpretation

**What you see:**

- A graph or other image. Section 4.2, "Data Displays," explains some kinds of graphics you might see.

- One or more statements with missing parts. Each missing part has a drop-down menu.

**Example of graphics:**

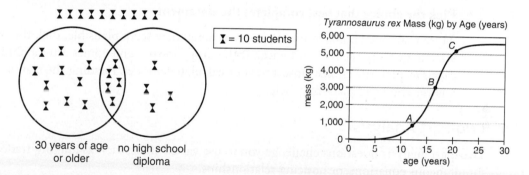

**Example of statement with blank/missing information and drop-down menus:**

Use the drop-down menus to complete each statement according to the information presented in the diagram.

If one student is selected at random from the 300 surveyed, the chance that the student will be under 30 or a high school graduate or both is [Select... ▾]

If one student is selected at random from the 300 surveyed, the chance that the student will be both under 30 and high school graduate is [1 out of 3 ▾]

| Select... |
|---|
| 1 out of 6 |
| 1 out of 3 |
| 2 out of 3 |
| 5 out of 6 |

**The response type:**

- Each drop-down menu shows a list of choices such as words, phrases, or numbers. Pick the best choice in the drop-down menu to fill in the missing part of the statement.

  - If the question has two or more drop-down menus, you must pick the best choices in all of them to get credit for the question.

## Tips for Answering Graphics Interpretation Questions

- **Study the graphic.**

  Find the information in the graphic. Notice any marked values on the axes. Also notice any differences between units in the graphic and units the text discusses. Don't assume the graphic is drawn to scale.

- **Read any text around the graphic.**

  Text near the graphic may clarify what the graphic means. The text may also give information that's not in the graphic but is needed to answer the question.

- **Study the statements with drop-down menus.**

  Studying these statements helps you understand what the question is asking you to do. Graphics interpretation questions may ask you to interpret and connect data, to find how different pieces of data are related, or to draw conclusions from a data set. You may have to do some math, for example to find or compare rates of change.

- **Read all the choices in each drop-down menu.**

  The menu choices may have clues about how to answer the question.

- **Pick the choice that best completes the statement.**

  More than one choice in the drop-down menu may seem plausible. Pick the one that makes the statement most accurate or logical. If the drop-down menu comes after a phrase like *nearest to* or *closest to*, pick the choice closest to your calculated answer. Reading the statement again with your answer choice in place may help.

## 4. Two-Part Analysis

Two-part analysis questions challenge you to use varied skills, such as judging trade-offs, solving simultaneous equations, or noticing relationships.

**What you see:**

- A written scenario.

- Instructions asking you to use the scenario to make two choices that together or separately meet one or more conditions.

- A response table with three columns.

**Example of a written scenario:**

A literature department at a small university in an English-speaking country is organizing a two-day festival in which it will highlight the works of ten writers who have been the subjects of recent scholarly work by the faculty. Five writers will be featured each day. To reflect the department's strengths, the majority of writers scheduled for one of the days will be writers whose primary writing language is not English. On the other day of the festival, at least four of the writers will be women. Neither day should have more than two writers from the same country. Departmental members have already agreed on a schedule for eight of the writers. That schedule showing names, along with each writer's primary writing language and country of origin, is shown.

- Day 1:

    Achebe (male, English, Nigeria)

    Weil (female, French, France)

    Gavalda (female, French, France)

    Barrett Browning (female, English, UK)

- Day 2:

    Rowling (female, English, UK)

    Austen (female, English, UK)

    Ocantos (male, Spanish, Argentina)

    Lu Xun (male, Chinese, China)

**Example of a response based on passage information:**

Select a writer who could be added to the schedule for either day. Then select a writer who could be added to the schedule for neither day. Make only two selections, one in each column.

| Either day | Neither day | Writer |
|:---:|:---:|---|
| ○ | ○ | LeGuin (female, English, USA) |
| ○ | ○ | Longfellow (make, English, USA) |
| ○ | ○ | Murasaki (female, Japanese, Japan) |
| ○ | ○ | Colette (female, French, France) |
| ○ | ○ | Vargas Llosa (male, Spanish, Peru) |
| ○ | ○ | Zola (male, French, France) |

## The response type:

- In the response table, the top row labels the columns. Below that, the first two columns have buttons you click to choose from a list in the third column.

- Pick one answer PER COLUMN, not per row.

    - To get credit for the question, you must pick one correct answer in the first column, and one in the second column.

    - You can pick the same answer in both columns.

## Tips for Answering Two-Part Analysis Questions

- **Answer using only the information given.**

    The question tells you everything you need to know to pick the right answers. Use only the information given as part of the question rather than any knowledge you already have on the topic to answer.

- **Read the instructions below the written scenario.**

    The table's top row may not fully explain the tasks in the first two columns. Carefully read how the instructions describe the tasks.

- **Make exactly two choices.**

    Pick one answer in the first column and one answer in the second column.

- **Read all the answer choices before picking any.**

  Before you pick answers in the first two columns, read all the answer choices in the third column.

- **Notice if the instructions say the two answers depend on each other.**

  Some two-part analysis questions ask you to make two independent choices. Others ask you to pick two answers that combine into a single correct response. Follow the instructions to make sure your two answer choices combine the right way.

- **Pick the same answer in both columns if it is the best choice for both.**

  Sometimes the same answer is the best choice for both columns.

## 5. Data Sufficiency

Like Quantitative Reasoning questions, Data Sufficiency questions use the basic math reviewed in Chapter 3, "Math Review." A Data Sufficiency question asks you to analyze a math problem, decide whether given information is relevant, and tell if enough information is given to solve the problem. But it doesn't ask you to find the problem's solution. Instead, you classify the problem by picking one of five answer choices. These five choices are the same for each question.

**What you see:**

- A math problem, sometimes with background information.
- Two statements labeled (1) and (2).

**Example of a Data Sufficiency Math Problem and Statements**

In Mr. Smith's class, what is the ratio of the number of boys to the number of girls?

(1) There are 3 times as many girls as boys in Mr. Smith's class.

(2) The number of boys is $\frac{1}{4}$ of the total number of boys and girls in Mr. Smith's class.

**The response type:**

- Each question is multiple choice, always with these five answer choices:

  (A)  Statement (1) ALONE is sufficient, but statement (2) alone is not sufficient.

  (B)  Statement (2) ALONE is sufficient, but statement (1) alone is not sufficient.

  (C)  BOTH statements TOGETHER are sufficient, but NEITHER statement ALONE is sufficient.

  (D)  EACH statement ALONE is sufficient.

  (E)  Statements (1) and (2) TOGETHER are NOT sufficient.

Pick exactly one of these answer choices. To answer correctly, you must judge whether statement (1) alone gives enough information to solve the math problem, and whether statement (2) alone does. If neither statement alone gives enough information to solve the problem, you must judge whether both do.

### Tips for Answering Data Sufficiency Questions

• **Analyze the math problem and the two statements step by step.**

First read the math problem and any background information. Then read statement (1). Decide whether it gives enough information to solve the problem. Now go on to statement (2). Ignore statement (1) while you decide whether statement (2) alone gives enough information to solve the problem. If you have found that either statement alone gives enough information to solve the problem, you now know enough to pick the right answer choice from among (A), (B), and (D).

If you find that neither statement alone gives enough information to solve the problem, decide whether both give enough information together. If so, the right answer choice is (C). Otherwise, it's (E).

Here's a flowchart showing how to find the right answer choice step by step.

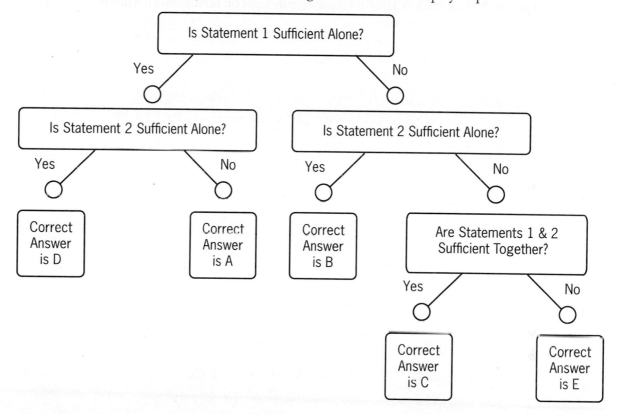

• **Don't waste time solving the math problem.**

You only have to decide whether the two statements give enough information to solve it.

• **Check whether there's enough information to solve the exact problem given.**

For example, suppose the problem is to find the value of a variable $y$. Then you have to decide whether each statement gives enough information to find **one and only one** value for $y$. Here, the question is not whether the statements just give enough information to find an equation like $y = x + 2$. Nor is it whether they give enough information to find a range of values rather than $y$'s exact value. So, ignore those irrelevant questions.

• **Don't assume any images are drawn to scale.**

They may not be. For example, if a figure described as a rectangle looks like a square, that doesn't mean it is a square.

# 5.3 Section Instructions

Go to **www.mba.com/tutorial** to read instructions for the section and get a feel for what the test center screens look like on the actual GMAT exam.

## More Data Insights Samples

For more sample questions of each type, visit: **mba.com/ir-questions**

## More Data Insights Practice

Below are Data Insights practice questions. Use your unique access code from the inside front cover of this book to access additional practice questions with answer explanations at **mba.com/my-account**. You can buy more Data Insights practice questions on **mba.com/gmatprep**.

# 5.4 Practice Questions

Each Data Sufficiency question has a math problem and two statements, labeled (1) and (2), which present data. Using this data with your knowledge of math and everyday facts (such as the number of days in July or what *counter-clockwise* means), decide whether the data in the statements are enough to solve the problem. Then pick one of these answer choices:

A    Statement (1) ALONE is sufficient, but statement (2) alone is not sufficient.
B    Statement (2) ALONE is sufficient, but statement (1) alone is not sufficient.
C    BOTH statements TOGETHER are sufficient, but NEITHER statement ALONE is sufficient.
D    EACH statement ALONE is sufficient.
E    Statements (1) and (2) TOGETHER are not sufficient.

<u>Note:</u> In Data Sufficiency questions that ask for a quantity's value, the data given in the statements are sufficient only when they make it possible to find exactly one numerical value for the quantity.

## Questions 1 to 31 - Difficulty: Easy

1.    Each car at a certain dealership is either blue or white. What is the average (arithmetic mean) sticker price of all the cars at the dealership?

   (1)   Of all the cars at the dealership, $\frac{1}{3}$ are blue and have an average sticker price of $21,000.

   (2)   Of all the cars at the dealership, $\frac{2}{3}$ are white and have an average sticker price of $24,000.

2.    A box contains only white balls and black balls. What is the probability that a ball selected at random from the box is white?

   (1)   There are 100 balls in the box.

   (2)   There are 40 black balls in the box.

3.    Rita's monthly salary is $\frac{2}{3}$ Juanita's monthly salary. What is their combined monthly salary?

   (1)   Rita's monthly salary is $4,000.

   (2)   Either Rita's monthly salary or Juanita's monthly salary is $6,000.

4.    Each of the 120 students in a certain dormitory is either a junior or a senior. How many of the juniors have credit cards?

   (1)   $\frac{2}{3}$ of the 120 juniors and seniors have credit cards.

   (2)   The number of seniors who have credit cards is 20 more than the number of juniors who have credit cards.

5.    If the average (arithmetic mean) cost per sweater for 3 pullover sweaters and 1 cardigan sweater was $65, what was the cost of the cardigan sweater?

   (1)   The average cost per sweater for the 3 pullover sweaters was $55.

   (2)   The most expensive of the 3 pullover sweaters cost $30 more than the least expensive.

6.    In each quarter of 1998, Company M earned more money than in the previous quarter. What was the range of Company M's quarterly earnings in 1998?

   (1)   In the 2nd and 3rd quarters of 1998, Company M earned $4.0 million and $4.6 million, respectively.

   (2)   In the 1st and 4th quarters of 1998, Company M earned $3.8 million and $4.9 million, respectively.

7. The range of the heights of a group of high school juniors and seniors is 20 centimeters. What is the average (arithmetic mean) of the height of the tallest senior in the group and the height of the shortest junior in the group?

    (1) The average of the heights of the juniors in the group is 165 centimeters.

    (2) The average of the heights of the seniors in the group is 179 centimeters.

8. In a certain factory, hours worked by each employee in excess of 40 hours per week are overtime hours and are paid for at $1\frac{1}{2}$ times the employee's regular hourly pay rate. If an employee worked a total of 42 hours last week, how much was the employee's gross pay for the hours worked last week?

    (1) The employee's gross pay for overtime hours worked last week was $30.

    (2) The employee's gross pay for all hours worked last week was $30 more than for the previous week.

9. Did Insurance Company K have more than $300 million in total net profits last year?

    (1) Last year Company K paid out $0.95 in claims for every dollar of premiums collected.

    (2) Last year Company K earned a total of $150 million in profits from the investment of accumulated surplus premiums from previous years.

10. How many hours would it take Pump A and Pump B working together, each at its own constant rate, to empty a tank that was initially full?

    (1) Working alone at its constant rate, Pump A would empty the full tank in 4 hours 20 minutes.

    (2) Working alone, Pump B would empty the full tank at its constant rate of 72 liters per minute.

11. Maria left home $\frac{1}{4}$ hour after her husband and drove over the same route as he had in order to overtake him. From the time she left, how many hours did it take Maria to overtake her husband?

    (1) Maria drove 60 miles before overtaking her husband.

    (2) While overtaking her husband, Maria drove at an average rate of 60 miles per hour, which was 12 miles per hour faster than her husband's average rate.

12. In a school that had a total of 600 students enrolled in the junior and senior classes, the students contributed to a certain fund. If all of the juniors but only half of the seniors contributed, was the total amount contributed more than $740 ?

    (1) Each junior contributed $1 and each senior who contributed gave $3.

    (2) There were more juniors than seniors enrolled in the school.

13. How much did credit-card fraud cost United States banks in year X to the nearest $10 million?

    (1) In year X, counterfeit cards and telephone and mail-order fraud accounted for 39 percent of the total amount that card fraud cost the banks.

    (2) In year X, stolen cards accounted for $158.4 million, or 16 percent, of the total amount that credit-card fraud cost the banks.

14. Company X's profits this year increased by 25% over last year's profits. Was the dollar amount of Company X's profits this year greater than the dollar amount of Company Y's?

    (1) Last year, the ratio of Company Y's profits to Company X's profits was 5:2.

    (2) Company Y experienced a 40% drop in profits from last year to this year.

15. A certain company consists of three divisions, A, B, and C. Of the employees in the three divisions, the employees in Division C have the greatest average (arithmetic mean) annual salary. Is the average annual salary of the employees in the three divisions combined less than $55,000 ?

    (1) The average annual salary of the employees in Divisions A and B combined is $45,000.

    (2) The average annual salary of the employees in Division C is $55,000.

16. A candle company determines that, for a certain specialty candle, the supply function is $p = m_1x + b_1$ and the demand function is $p = m_2x + b_2$, where $p$ is the price of each candle, $x$ is the number of candles supplied or demanded, and $m_1$, $m_2$, $b_1$, and $b_2$ are constants. At what value of $x$ do the graphs of the supply function and demand function intersect?

    (1) $m_1 = -m_2 = 0.005$

    (2) $b_2 - b_1 = 6$

17. A certain ski shop sold 125 pairs of skis and 100 pairs of ski boots for a total of $75,000. What was the average (arithmetic mean) selling price of a pair of the ski boots?

    (1) The average selling price of a pair of skis was $300.

    (2) The selling price of a pair of ski boots varied from $150 to $900.

18. Last year Publisher X published 1,100 books, consisting of first editions, revised editions, and reprints. How many first editions did Publisher X publish last year?

    (1) The number of first editions published was 50 more than twice the number of reprints published.

    (2) The number of revised editions published was half the number of reprints published.

19. How old is Jane?

    (1) Ten years ago she was one-third as old as she is now.

    (2) In 15 years, she will be twice as old as she is now.

20. What was the population of City X in 2002 ?

    (1) X's population in 2002 increased by 2 percent, or 20,000 people, over 2001.

    (2) In 2001, X's population was 1,000,000.

21. Yesterday Bookstore B sold twice as many softcover books as hardcover books. Was Bookstore B's revenue from the sale of softcover books yesterday greater than its revenue from the sale of hardcover books yesterday?

    (1) The average (arithmetic mean) price of the hardcover books sold at the store yesterday was $10 more than the average price of the softcover books sold at the store yesterday.

    (2) The average price of the softcover and hardcover books sold at the store yesterday was greater than $14.

22. A customer purchased 6 shirts priced at $10.99 each, excluding sales tax. How much sales tax did he pay on this purchase?

    (1) The customer paid a 5 percent sales tax on the total price of the shirts.

    (2) The customer paid a total of $11.54 for each shirt, including sales tax.

23. The sum of the lengths of two pieces of rope is 65 feet. How long is the shorter piece?

    (1) The lengths of the pieces of rope are in the ratio $8 : 5$.

    (2) One piece of rope is 15 feet longer than the other piece.

24. An initial investment of $10,000 was deposited in a bank account one year ago, and additional deposits were made during the year. If no withdrawals were made, what was the total amount of interest earned on this account during the year?

    (1) The additional deposits during the year totaled $5,000.

    (2) The account earned interest at the annual rate of 6 percent compounded quarterly.

25. A poplar tree was 3 feet high when it was planted on January 1, 1970. During what year did it pass the height of 20 feet?

    (1) On January 1, 1973, it was 24 feet high.

    (2) It doubled its height during each year.

26. Which weighs more, a cubic unit of water or a cubic unit of liquid X ?

    (1) A cubic unit of water weighs more than $\frac{1}{3}$ cubic unit of liquid X.

    (2) A cubic unit of liquid X weighs less than 3 cubic units of water.

27. What were the individual prices of the vases that an antique dealer bought at store *X* ?

    (1) The antique dealer bought exactly 3 vases at store *X*.

    (2) The antique dealer's total bill at store *X* was $225.

28. Was the average (arithmetic mean) sale price of a new home in region *R* last month at least $100,000 ?

    (1) Last month the median sale price of a new home in region *R* was at least $100,000.

    (2) Last month the sale prices of new homes in region *R* ranged from $75,000 to $150,000.

29. If the capacity of tank X is less than the capacity of tank Y and both tanks begin to fill at the same time, which tank will be filled first?

    (1) Tank X is filled at a constant rate of 1.5 liters per minute.

    (2) Tank Y is filled at a constant rate of 120 liters per hour.

30. At a certain company, 30 percent of the employees live in City R. If 25 percent of the company's employees live in apartments in City R, what is the number of the employees who live in apartments in City R?

    (1) Of the employees who live in City R, 6 do not live in apartments.

    (2) Of the employees, 84 do not live in City R.

31. What was Mary's average (arithmetic mean) score on 4 tests?

    (1) Her average (arithmetic mean) score on 3 of the tests was 97.

    (2) Her score on one of the tests was 96.

## Questions 32 to 59 - Difficulty: Medium

|          | Yes | No  | Don't Know |
|----------|-----|-----|------------|
| Program X | 400 | 200 | 400 |
| Program Y | 300 | 350 | 350 |

32. The table shows the number of people who responded "yes" or "no" or "don't know" when asked whether their city council should implement environmental programs X and Y. If a total of 1,000 people responded to the question about both programs, what was the number of people who did not respond "yes" to implementing either of the two programs?

    (1) The number of people who responded "yes" to implementing only Program X was 300.

    (2) The number of people who responded "no" to implementing Program X and "no" to implementing Program Y was 100.

33. An estimate of an actual data value has an error of *p* percent if $p = \dfrac{100|e-a|}{a}$, where *e* is the estimated value and *a* is the actual value. Emma's estimate for her total income last year had an error of less than 20 percent. Emma's estimate of her income from tutoring last year also had an error of less than 20 percent. Was Emma's actual income from tutoring last year at most 45 percent of her actual total income last year?

    (1) Emma's estimated income last year from tutoring was 30 percent of her estimated total income last year.

    (2) Emma's estimated total income last year was $40,000.

34. Was Store K's profit last month at least 10 percent greater than its profit the previous month?

    (1) Store K's expenses last month were 5 percent greater than its expenses the previous month.

    (2) Store K's revenues last month were 10 percent greater than its revenues the previous month.

35. Gross profit is equal to selling price minus cost. A car dealer's gross profit on the sale of a certain car was what percent of the cost of the car?

(1) The selling price of the car was $\frac{11}{10}$ of the cost of the car.

(2) The cost of the car was $14,500.

36. When the wind speed is 9 miles per hour, the wind-chill factor $w$ is given by

$$w = -17.366 + 1.19t,$$

where $t$ is the temperature in degrees Fahrenheit. If at noon yesterday the wind speed was 9 miles per hour, was the wind-chill factor greater than 0 ?

(1) The temperature at noon yesterday was greater than 10 degrees Fahrenheit.

(2) The temperature at noon yesterday was less than 20 degrees Fahrenheit.

37. How many members of a certain legislature voted against the measure to raise their salaries?

(1) $\frac{1}{4}$ of the members of the legislature did not vote on the measure.

(2) If 5 additional members of the legislature had voted against the measure, then the fraction of members of the legislature voting against the measure would have been $\frac{1}{3}$.

38. During a certain bicycle ride, was Sherry's average speed faster than 24 kilometers per hour?
(1 kilometer = 1,000 meters)

(1) Sherry's average speed during the bicycle ride was faster than 7 meters per second.

(2) Sherry's average speed during the bicycle ride was slower than 8 meters per second.

39. Working together, Rafael and Salvador can tabulate a certain set of data in 2 hours. In how many hours can Rafael tabulate the data working alone?

(1) Working alone, Rafael can tabulate the data in 3 hours less time than Salvador, working alone, can tabulate the data.

(2) Working alone, Rafael can tabulate the data in $\frac{1}{2}$ the time that Salvador, working alone, can tabulate the data.

40. Yesterday between 9:00 a.m. and 6:00 p.m. at Airport X, all flights to Atlanta departed at equally spaced times and all flights to New York City departed at equally spaced times. A flight to Atlanta and a flight to New York City both departed from Airport X at 1:00 p.m. yesterday. Between 1:00 p.m. and 3:00 p.m. yesterday, did another pair of flights to these 2 cities depart from Airport X at the same time?

(1) Yesterday at Airport X, a flight to Atlanta and a flight to New York City both departed at 10:00 a.m.

(2) Yesterday at Airport X, flights to New York City departed every 15 minutes between 9:00 a.m. and 6:00 p.m.

41. Of the total number of copies of Magazine X sold last week, 40 percent were sold at full price. What was the total number of copies of the magazine sold last week?

(1) Last week, full price for a copy of Magazine X was $1.50 and the total revenue from full-price sales was $112,500.

(2) The total number of copies of Magazine X sold last week at full price was $75,000.

42. What is the average (arithmetic mean) annual salary of the 6 employees of a toy company?

(1) If the 6 annual salaries were ordered from least to greatest, each annual salary would be $6,300 greater than the preceding annual salary.

(2) The range of the 6 annual salaries is $31,500.

43. In a certain order, the pretax price of each regular pencil was $0.03, the pretax price of each deluxe pencil was $0.05, and there were 50% more deluxe pencils than regular pencils. All taxes on the order are a fixed percent of the pretax prices. The sum of the total pretax price of the order and the tax on the order was $44.10. What was the amount, in dollars, of the tax on the order?

(1) The tax on the order was 5% of the total pretax price of the order.

(2) The order contained exactly 400 regular pencils.

44. A total of 20 amounts are entered on a spreadsheet that has 5 rows and 4 columns; each of the 20 positions in the spreadsheet contains one amount. The average (arithmetic mean) of the amounts in row $i$ is $R_i$ ($1 \leq i \leq 5$). The average of the amounts in column $j$ is $C_j$ ($1 \leq j \leq 4$). What is the average of all 20 amounts on the spreadsheet?

    (1) $R_1 + R_2 + R_3 + R_4 + R_5 = 550$
    (2) $C_1 + C_2 + C_3 + C_4 = 440$

45. Was the range of the amounts of money that Company Y budgeted for its projects last year equal to the range of the amounts of money that it budgeted for its projects this year?

    (1) Both last year and this year, Company Y budgeted money for 12 projects and the least amount of money that it budgeted for a project was $400.
    (2) Both last year and this year, the average (arithmetic mean) amount of money that Company Y budgeted per project was $2,000.

46. What is the probability that Lee will make exactly 5 errors on a certain typing test?

    (1) The probability that Lee will make 5 or more errors on the test is 0.27.
    (2) The probability that Lee will make 5 or fewer errors on the test is 0.85.

47. A small factory that produces only upholstered chairs and sofas uses 1 cushion for each chair and 4 cushions for each sofa. If the factory used a total of 300 cushions on the furniture it produced last week, how many sofas did it produce last week?

    (1) Last week the factory produced more chairs than sofas.
    (2) Last week the factory produced a total of 150 chairs and sofas.

DISTRIBUTION OF SALESPERSONS
BY GENDER IN THREE SECTORS, YEAR $X$

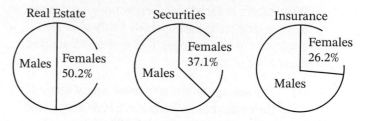

48. In year $X$ were there more female salespersons in the securities sector than in the insurance sector?

    (1) There were more male salespersons in the insurance sector than in the securities sector.
    (2) The total number of salespersons was greater in the securities sector than in the insurance sector.

49. If a club made a gross profit of $0.25 for each candy bar it sold, how many candy bars did the club sell?

    (1) The total revenue from the sale of the candy bars was $300.
    (2) If the club had sold 80 more candy bars, its gross profits would have increased by 20 percent.

50. In one year 2,100 malpractice claims were filed with insurance company X and of these $\frac{1}{4}$ resulted in a financial settlement. Of those resulting in a financial settlement of less than $400,000, what was the average payment per claim?

    (1) Company X paid a total of 24.5 million dollars to the claimants.
    (2) Only 5 claims resulted in payments of $400,000 or more.

51. If there are 13 boys in club X, what is the average age of these boys?

    (1) The oldest boy is 13 years old and the youngest boy is 9 years old.
    (2) Eleven of the boys are either 10 years old or 11 years old.

52. If all the employees of a company fall into one and only one of 3 groups, X, Y, or Z, with 250, 100, and 20 members in each group, respectively, what is the average (arithmetic mean) weekly salary of all the employees of this company, if all employees are paid every week of the year?

   (1) The average (arithmetic mean) annual salary of the employees in Group X is $10,000, in Group Y $15,000 and in Group Z $20,000.

   (2) The total annual payroll is $4,400,000.

DISTRIBUTION OF SALES INCOME
FOR STORE *S* LAST WEEK

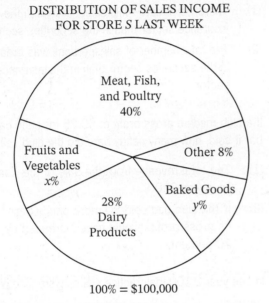

100% = $100,000

53. According to the graph above, the sale of fruits and vegetables in Store *S* last week accounted for what percent of the total sales income for the week?

   (1) Last week the total income from the sale of fruits and vegetables in Store *S* was $16,000.

   (2) $x = 2y$

54. Larry saves *x* dollars per month. Will Larry's total savings one year from now exceed his present savings by at least $500 ? (Assume that there is no interest.)

   (1) In 6 months Larry's total savings will be $900.

   (2) In 3 months Larry's total savings will exceed his present savings by $150.

55. If Randy has twice as many coins as Alice, and if Maria has 7 times as many coins as Alice, what is the combined number of coins that all three of them have?

   (1) Alice has 4 fewer coins than Randy.

   (2) Maria has 20 more coins than Randy.

56. A line of people waiting to enter a theater consists of seven separate and successive groups. The first person in each group purchases one ticket for each person in the group and for no one else. If *n* is the total number of tickets sold for the first six groups, is *n* an even number?

   (1) There are no more than 4 people in each group.

   (2) The 19th person in line purchases the tickets for the seventh group.

57. If John has exactly 10 coins each of which was minted in 1910 or 1920 or 1930, how many of his coins were minted in 1920 ?

   (1) Exactly 6 of his coins were minted in 1910 or 1920.

   (2) Exactly 7 of his coins were minted in 1920 or 1930.

58. The total profit of corporation K was $3,400,000 in year X. What was the total profit in year Y ?

   (1) Income in year Y was 30 percent more than in year X.

   (2) Costs in year Y were 40 percent more than in year X.

59. Zelma scored 90, 88, and 92 on 3 of the 6 mathematics tests that she took. What was her average (arithmetic mean) score on the 6 tests?

   (1) Her average (arithmetic mean) score on 5 of the tests was 90.

   (2) Her score on one of the tests was 91.

## Questions 60 to 83 - Difficulty: **Hard**

60. What percent of the students at University X are enrolled in a science course but are not enrolled in a biology course?

    (1) 28 percent of the students at University X are enrolled in a biology course.

    (2) 70 percent of the students at University X who are enrolled in a science course are enrolled in a biology course.

61. Each Type A machine fills 400 cans per minute, each Type B machine fills 600 cans per minute, and each Type C machine installs 2,400 lids per minute. A lid is installed on each can that is filled and on no can that is not filled. For a particular minute, what is the total number of machines working?

    (1) A total of 4,800 cans are filled that minute.

    (2) For that minute, there are 2 Type B machines working for every Type C machine working.

62. In a two-month survey of shoppers, each shopper bought one of two brands of detergent, X or Y, in the first month and again bought one of these brands in the second month. In the survey, 90 percent of the shoppers who bought Brand X in the first month bought Brand X again in the second month, while 60 percent of the shoppers who bought Brand Y in the first month bought Brand Y again in the second month. What percent of the shoppers bought Brand Y in the second month?

    (1) In the first month, 50 percent of the shoppers bought Brand X.

    (2) The total number of shoppers surveyed was 5,000.

63. If the total price of $n$ equally priced shares of a certain stock was $12,000, what was the price per share of the stock?

    (1) If the price per share of the stock had been $1 more, the total price of the $n$ shares would have been $300 more.

    (2) If the price per share of the stock had been $2 less, the total price of the $n$ shares would have been 5 percent less.

64. In Year X, 8.7 percent of the men in the labor force were unemployed in June compared with 8.4 percent in May. If the number of men in the labor force was the same for both months, how many men were unemployed in June of that year?

    (1) In May of Year X, the number of unemployed men in the labor force was 3.36 million.

    (2) In Year X, 120,000 more men in the labor force were unemployed in June than in May.

65. On Monday morning a certain machine ran continuously at a uniform rate to fill a production order. At what time did it completely fill the order that morning?

    (1) The machine began filling the order at 9:30 a.m.

    (2) The machine had filled $\frac{1}{2}$ of the order by 10:30 a.m. and $\frac{5}{6}$ of the order by 11:10 a.m.

66. After winning 50 percent of the first 20 games it played, Team A won all of the remaining games it played. What was the total number of games that Team A won?

    (1) Team A played 25 games altogether.

    (2) Team A won 60 percent of all the games it played.

67. Michael arranged all his books in a bookcase with 10 books on each shelf and no books left over. After Michael acquired 10 additional books, he arranged all his books in a new bookcase with 12 books on each shelf and no books left over. How many books did Michael have before he acquired the 10 additional books?

    (1) Before Michael acquired the 10 additional books, he had fewer than 96 books.

    (2) Before Michael acquired the 10 additional books, he had more than 24 books.

68. Last year in a group of 30 businesses, 21 reported a net profit and 15 had investments in foreign markets. How many of the businesses did not report a net profit nor invest in foreign markets last year?

    (1) Last year 12 of the 30 businesses reported a net profit and had investments in foreign markets.

    (2) Last year 24 of the 30 businesses reported a net profit or invested in foreign markets, or both.

69. For each landscaping job that takes more than 4 hours, a certain contractor charges a total of r dollars for the first 4 hours plus 0.2r dollars for each additional hour or fraction of an hour, where r > 100. Did a particular landscaping job take more than 10 hours?

    (1) The contractor charged a total of $288 for the job.

    (2) The contractor charged a total of 2.4r dollars for the job.

70. If 75 percent of the guests at a certain banquet ordered dessert, what percent of the guests ordered coffee?

    (1) 60 percent of the guests who ordered dessert also ordered coffee.

    (2) 90 percent of the guests who ordered coffee also ordered dessert.

71. A tank containing water started to leak. Did the tank contain more than 30 gallons of water when it started to leak? (Note: 1 gallon = 128 ounces)

    (1) The water leaked from the tank at a constant rate of 6.4 ounces per minute.

    (2) The tank became empty less than 12 hours after it started to leak.

72. Each of the 45 books on a shelf is written either in English or in Spanish, and each of the books is either a hardcover book or a paperback. If a book is to be selected at random from the books on the shelf, is the probability less than $\frac{1}{2}$ that the book selected will be a paperback written in Spanish?

    (1) Of the books on the shelf, 30 are paperbacks.

    (2) Of the books on the shelf, 15 are written in Spanish.

73. A small school has three foreign language classes, one in French, one in Spanish, and one in German. How many of the 34 students enrolled in the Spanish class are also enrolled in the French class?

    (1) There are 27 students enrolled in the French class, and 49 students enrolled in either the French class, the Spanish class, or both of these classes.

    (2) One-half of the students enrolled in the Spanish class are enrolled in more than one foreign language class.

74. Last year $\frac{3}{5}$ of the members of a certain club were males. This year the members of the club include all the members from last year plus some new members. Is the fraction of the members of the club who are males greater this year than last year?

    (1) More than half of the new members are male.

    (2) The number of members of the club this year is $\frac{6}{5}$ the number of members last year.

75. Machines K, M, and N, each working alone at its constant rate, produce 1 widget in x, y, and 2 minutes, respectively. If Machines K, M, and N work simultaneously at their respective constant rates, does it take them less than 1 hour to produce a total of 50 widgets?

    (1) x < 1.5

    (2) y < 1.2

76. Stations X and Y are connected by two separate, straight, parallel rail lines that are 250 miles long. Train P and train Q simultaneously left Station X and Station Y, respectively, and each train traveled to the other's point of departure. The two trains passed each other after traveling for 2 hours. When the two trains passed, which train was nearer to its destination?

    (1) At the time when the two trains passed, train P had averaged a speed of 70 miles per hour.

    (2) Train Q averaged a speed of 55 miles per hour for the entire trip.

77. In a two-story apartment complex, each apartment on the upper floor rents for 75 percent as much as each apartment on the lower floor. If the total monthly rent is $15,300 when rent is collected on all of the apartments, what is the monthly rent on each apartment on the lower floor?

    (1) An apartment on the lower floor rents for $150 more per month than an apartment on the upper floor.

    (2) There are 6 more apartments on the upper floor than on the lower floor.

78. A motorboat, which is set to travel at $k$ kilometers per hour in still water, travels directly up and down the center of a straight river so that the change in the boat's speed relative to the shore depends only on the speed and direction of the current. What is the value of $k$?

    (1) It takes the same amount of time for the boat to travel 4 kilometers directly downstream as it takes for it to travel 3 kilometers directly upstream.

    (2) The current flows directly downstream at a constant rate of 2.5 kilometers per hour.

79. If the book value of a certain piece of equipment was $5,000 exactly 5 years ago, what is its present book value?

    (1) From the time the piece of equipment was purchased, its book value decreased by 10 percent of its purchase price each year of its life.

    (2) The present book value of another piece of equipment is $2,000.

80. The total cost to charter a bus was shared equally by the people who went on a certain trip. If the total cost to charter the bus was $360, how many people went on the trip?

    (1) Each person who went on the trip paid $9 to charter the bus.

    (2) If 4 fewer people had gone on the trip, each person's share of the total cost to charter the bus would have increased by $1.

81. If each of the stamps Carla bought cost 20, 25, or 30 cents and she bought at least one of each denomination, what is the number of 25-cent stamps that she bought?

    (1) She spent a total of $1.45 for stamps.

    (2) She bought exactly 6 stamps.

82. A car traveled a distance of $d$ miles in $t$ minutes at an average rate of $r$ miles per minute. What is the ratio of $d$ to $r$?

    (1) $t = 30$

    (2) $d = 25$

83. Pat is reading a book that has a total of 15 chapters. Has Pat read at least $\frac{1}{3}$ of the pages in the book?

    (1) Pat has just finished reading the first 5 chapters.

    (2) Each of the first 3 chapters has more pages than each of the other 12 chapters in the book.

# 5.5 Answer Key

| | | | | | | | |
|---|---|---|---|---|---|---|---|
| 1. | C | 18. | C | 35. | A | 52. | D |
| 2. | C | 19. | D | 36. | E | 53. | D |
| 3. | A | 20. | A | 37. | E | 54. | B |
| 4. | C | 21. | C | 38. | A | 55. | D |
| 5. | A | 22. | D | 39. | D | 56. | B |
| 6. | B | 23. | D | 40. | E | 57. | C |
| 7. | E | 24. | E | 41. | D | 58. | E |
| 8. | A | 25. | B | 42. | E | 59. | E |
| 9. | E | 26. | E | 43. | D | 60. | C |
| 10. | E | 27. | E | 44. | D | 61. | C |
| 11. | B | 28. | E | 45. | E | 62. | A |
| 12. | E | 29. | E | 46. | C | 63. | D |
| 13. | B | 30. | D | 47. | B | 64. | D |
| 14. | C | 31. | E | 48. | B | 65. | B |
| 15. | B | 32. | A | 49. | B | 66. | D |
| 16. | C | 33. | A | 50. | E | 67. | A |
| 17. | A | 34. | C | 51. | E | 68. | D |

| | |
|---|---|
| 69. | B |
| 70. | C |
| 71. | E |
| 72. | B |
| 73. | A |
| 74. | E |
| 75. | D |
| 76. | A |
| 77. | A |
| 78. | C |
| 79. | E |
| 80. | D |
| 81. | E |
| 82. | A |
| 83. | E |

# 5.6 Answer Explanations

The following discussion of Data Insights is intended to familiarize you with the most efficient and effective approaches to the kinds of problems common to Data Insights. The particular questions in this chapter are generally representative of the kinds of Data Insights questions you will encounter on the GMAT exam. Remember that it is the problem solving strategy that is important, not the specific details of a particular question.

## Questions 1 to 31 - Difficulty: Easy

1. Each car at a certain dealership is either blue or white. What is the average (arithmetic mean) sticker price of all the cars at the dealership?

    (1) Of all the cars at the dealership, $\frac{1}{3}$ are blue and have an average sticker price of $21,000.

    (2) Of all the cars at the dealership, $\frac{2}{3}$ are white and have an average sticker price of $24,000.

**Algebra** Statistics

Let $\Sigma_b$ and $\Sigma_w$ be the sum of the sticker prices, respectively and in dollars, of the blue cars and the white cars at the dealership, and let $n$ be the number of cars at the dealership. Determine the value of $\dfrac{\Sigma_b + \Sigma_w}{n}$.

(1) Given that there are $\frac{1}{3}n$ blue cars having an average sticker price of $21,000, it follows that $\Sigma_b = \left(\frac{1}{3}n\right)21,000 = 7,000n$. Therefore,

$$\frac{\Sigma_b + \Sigma_w}{n} = \frac{7,000n + \Sigma_w}{n} = 7,000 + \frac{\Sigma_w}{n},$$

which can have more than one possible value by suitably varying $\Sigma_w$ and $n$; NOT sufficient.

(2) Given that there are $\frac{2}{3}n$ white cars having an average sticker price of $24,000, it follows that $\Sigma_w = \left(\frac{2}{3}n\right)24,000 = 16,000n$. Therefore, $\dfrac{\Sigma_b + \Sigma_w}{n} = \dfrac{\Sigma_b + 16,000n}{n} =$

$\dfrac{\Sigma_b}{n} + 16,000$, which can have more than

one possible value by suitably varying $\Sigma_b$ and $n$; NOT sufficient.

Taking (1) and (2) together, $\dfrac{\Sigma_b + \Sigma_w}{n} =$

$\dfrac{7,000n + 16,000n}{n} = \dfrac{23,000n}{n} = 23,000.$

**The correct answer is C;
both statements together are sufficient.**

2. A box contains only white balls and black balls. What is the probability that a ball selected at random from the box is white?

    (1) There are 100 balls in the box.
    (2) There are 40 black balls in the box.

**Arithmetic** Probability

Determine the probability of selecting a white ball from a box that contains only white and black balls.

(1) Given that there are 100 balls in the box, it is impossible to determine the probability of selecting a white ball because there is no information on the white/black split of the 100 balls in the box; NOT sufficient.

(2) Given that there are 40 black balls in the box, it is impossible to determine the probability of selecting a white ball because there is no indication of either the total number of balls in the box or the number of white balls; NOT sufficient.

Taking (1) and (2) together, there are 100 balls in the box, 40 of which are black. It follows that the number of white balls is $100 - 40 = 60$ and the probability of selecting a white ball is $\dfrac{60}{100} = \dfrac{3}{5}$.

**The correct answer is C;
both statements together are sufficient.**

3. Rita's monthly salary is $\frac{2}{3}$ Juanita's monthly salary. What is their combined monthly salary?

(1) Rita's monthly salary is $4,000.

(2) Either Rita's monthly salary or Juanita's monthly salary is $6,000.

**Arithmetic Applied Problems**

Let $R$ and $J$ be Rita's and Juanita's monthly salaries, respectively, in dollars. It is given that $R = \frac{2}{3}J$. Determine the value of their combined salary, which can be expressed as $R + J = \frac{2}{3}J + J = \frac{5}{3}J$.

(1) Given that $R = 4,000$, it follows that $4,000 = \frac{2}{3}J$, or $J = \frac{3}{2}(4,000) = 6,000$. Therefore, $\frac{5}{3}J = \frac{5}{3}(6,000) = 10,000$; SUFFICIENT.

(2) Given that $R = 6,000$ or $J = 6,000$, then $J = \frac{3}{2}(6,000) = 9,000$ or $J = 6,000$. Thus, $\frac{5}{3}J = \frac{5}{3}(9,000) = 15,000$ or $\frac{5}{3}J = \frac{5}{3}(6,000) = 10,000$, and so it is not possible to determine the value of $\frac{5}{3}J$; NOT sufficient.

**The correct answer is A; statement 1 alone is sufficient.**

4. Each of the 120 students in a certain dormitory is either a junior or a senior. How many of the juniors have credit cards?

(1) $\frac{2}{3}$ of the 120 juniors and seniors have credit cards.

(2) The number of seniors who have credit cards is 20 more than the number of juniors who have credit cards.

**Algebra First-Degree Equations**

Determine the number of juniors who have credit cards among the 120 students in a certain junior/senior dormitory.

(1) Given that $\frac{2}{3}$ of the 120 students have credit cards, it follows that 80 students have credit cards. There is no information regarding the number of juniors in this group of 80; NOT sufficient.

(2) Given that the number of seniors with credit cards is 20 more than the number of juniors with credit cards, it is impossible to determine how many juniors have credit cards because no information is given about the junior/senior split nor about the have/do not have credit cards split of the 120 students; NOT sufficient.

Taking (1) and (2) together, 80 students have credit cards from (1) and the number of seniors with credit cards is 20 more than the number of juniors with credit cards from (2). Thus, $J + S = 80$ or $J + (J + 20) = 80$, which can be solved for a unique value of $J$.

**The correct answer is C; both statements together are sufficient.**

5. If the average (arithmetic mean) cost per sweater for 3 pullover sweaters and 1 cardigan sweater was $65, what was the cost of the cardigan sweater?

(1) The average cost per sweater for the 3 pullover sweaters was $55.

(2) The most expensive of the 3 pullover sweaters cost $30 more than the least expensive.

**Algebra Statistics**

Letting $P$ represent the average cost, in dollars, of 1 pullover sweater and $C$, the cost, in dollars, of the cardigan, it is given that $\frac{3P + C}{4} = 65$ or $3P + C = 260$. Determine the value of $C$.

(1) It is given that $P = 55$. Therefore, $3P = 3(55) = 165$ and $C = 260 - 165 = 95$; SUFFICIENT.

(2) Given that the most expensive pullover sweater cost $30 more than the least expensive, it is impossible to determine the value of $C$. For example, if the price of the most expensive pullover sweater was $60, the price of the least expensive was $30, and the price of the other pullover sweater was $40, then the value of $C = 260 - 60 - 30 - 40 = 130$. But if the price of the most expensive pullover sweater was $60, the price of the least expensive

was $30, and the price of the other pullover sweater was $50, then the value of $C = 260 - 60 - 30 - 50 = 120$; NOT sufficient.

**The correct answer is A; statement 1 alone is sufficient.**

6. In each quarter of 1998, Company M earned more money than in the previous quarter. What was the range of Company M's quarterly earnings in 1998?

    (1) In the 2nd and 3rd quarters of 1998, Company M earned $4.0 million and $4.6 million, respectively.

    (2) In the 1st and 4th quarters of 1998, Company M earned $3.8 million and $4.9 million, respectively.

**Arithmetic** Statistics

We know that for each of the quarters in 1998, Company M earned more money than in the previous quarter. Is it possible to determine the range of the company's quarterly earnings in 1998?

    (1) Although we are told the value of the earnings for the 2nd and 3rd quarters, Company M's 4th quarter earnings could, consistent with statement 1, be any amount that is greater than the 3rd quarter earnings. Likewise, the company's 1st quarter earnings could be any positive amount that is less than the company's 2nd quarter earnings. The difference between these two values would be the range, and we see that it cannot be determined; NOT sufficient.

    (2) We are given the earnings for the 1st and 4th quarters, and we already know that, from quarter to quarter, the earnings in 1998 have always increased. We can thus infer that Company M's earnings for the 2nd and 3rd quarters are less than the 4th quarter earnings but greater than the 1st quarter earnings. The difference between the greatest quarterly earnings and the least quarter earnings for 1998 is thus the difference between the 4th quarter earnings and the 1st quarter earnings—the values $4.9 million and $3.8 million, respectively, that we have been given; SUFFICIENT.

**The correct answer is B; statement 2 alone is sufficient.**

7. The range of the heights of a group of high school juniors and seniors is 20 centimeters. What is the average (arithmetic mean) of the height of the tallest senior in the group and the height of the shortest junior in the group?

    (1) The average of the heights of the juniors in the group is 165 centimeters.

    (2) The average of the heights of the seniors in the group is 179 centimeters.

**Arithmetic** Statistics

Determine the average of the height of the tallest senior and the height of the shortest junior.

    (1) Given that the average of the heights of the juniors is 165 cm, it is not possible to determine the average of the height of the tallest senior and the height of the shortest junior. For example, the heights of the juniors could all be 165 cm and there could be three seniors with heights 176 cm, 176 cm, and 185 cm. In this case the range of all the heights is $185 - 165 = 20$ cm, the average of the heights of the juniors is 165 cm, and the average of the height of the tallest senior and the height of the shortest junior is $\frac{185 + 165}{2} = 175$. On the other hand, the heights of the seniors could all be 179 cm and there could be three juniors with heights 159 cm, 168 cm, and 168 cm. In this case the range of all the heights is $179 - 159 = 20$ cm, the average of the heights of the juniors is 165 cm, and the average of the height of the tallest senior and the height of the shortest junior is $\frac{179 + 159}{2} = 169$; NOT sufficient.

    (2) Given that the average of the heights of the seniors is 179 cm, it is not possible to determine the average of the height of the tallest senior and the height of the shortest junior because, for each of the examples used in (1) above, the average of the heights of the seniors is 179 cm; NOT sufficient.

Taking (1) and (2) together, it is not possible to determine the average of the height of the tallest senior and the height of the shortest junior because each of the examples used in (1) above satisfies both (1) and (2).

**The correct answer is E;
both statements together are still not sufficient.**

8. In a certain factory, hours worked by each employee in excess of 40 hours per week are overtime hours and are paid for at $1\frac{1}{2}$ times the employee's regular hourly pay rate. If an employee worked a total of 42 hours last week, how much was the employee's gross pay for the hours worked last week?

   (1) The employee's gross pay for overtime hours worked last week was $30.

   (2) The employee's gross pay for all hours worked last week was $30 more than for the previous week.

**Arithmetic Applied Problems**

If an employee's regular hourly rate was $R$ and the employee worked 42 hours last week, then the employee's gross pay for hours worked last week was $40R + 2(1.5R)$. Determine the value of $40R + 2(1.5R) = 43R$, or equivalently, the value of $R$.

   (1) Given that the employee's gross pay for overtime hours worked last week was $30, it follows that $2(1.5R) = 30$ and $R = 10$; SUFFICIENT.

   (2) Given that the employee's gross pay for all hours worked last week was $30 more than for the previous week, the value of $R$ cannot be determined because nothing specific is known about the value of the employee's pay for all hours worked the previous week; NOT sufficient.

**The correct answer is A;
statement 1 alone is sufficient.**

9. Did Insurance Company K have more than $300 million in total net profits last year?

   (1) Last year Company K paid out $0.95 in claims for every dollar of premiums collected.

   (2) Last year Company K earned a total of $150 million in profits from the investment of accumulated surplus premiums from previous years.

**Arithmetic Applied Problems**

Letting $R$ and $E$, respectively, represent the company's total revenue and total expenses last year, determine if $R - E > \$300$ million.

   (1) This indicates that, for $\$x$ in premiums collected, the company paid $\$0.95x$ in claims, but gives no information about other sources of revenue or other types of expenses; NOT sufficient.

   (2) This indicates that the company's profits from the investment of accumulated surplus premiums was $150 million last year, but gives no information about other sources of revenue or other types of expenses; NOT sufficient.

Taking (1) and (2) together gives information on profit resulting from collecting premiums and paying claims as well as profit resulting from investments from accumulated surplus premiums, but gives no indication whether there were other sources of revenue or other types of expenses.

**The correct answer is E;
both statements together are still not sufficient.**

10. How many hours would it take Pump A and Pump B working together, each at its own constant rate, to empty a tank that was initially full?

   (1) Working alone at its constant rate, Pump A would empty the full tank in 4 hours 20 minutes.

   (2) Working alone, Pump B would empty the full tank at its constant rate of 72 liters per minute.

**Arithmetic Applied Problems**

Determine how long it would take Pumps A and B working together, each at its own constant rate, to empty a full tank.

   (1) This indicates how long it would take Pump A to empty the tank, but gives no information about Pump B's constant rate; NOT sufficient.

   (2) This indicates the rate at which Pump B can empty the tank, but without information about the capacity of the tank or Pump A's rate, it is not possible to determine how long both pumps working together would take to empty the tank; NOT sufficient.

Taking (1) and (2) together gives the amount of time it would take Pump A to empty the tank and the rate at which Pump B can empty the tank, but without knowing the capacity of the tank, it is not possible to determine how long the pumps working together would take to empty the tank.

**The correct answer is E;
both statements together are still not sufficient.**

11. Maria left home $\frac{1}{4}$ hour after her husband and drove over the same route as he had in order to overtake him. From the time she left, how many hours did it take Maria to overtake her husband?

(1) Maria drove 60 miles before overtaking her husband.

(2) While overtaking her husband, Maria drove at an average rate of 60 miles per hour, which was 12 miles per hour faster than her husband's average rate.

**Arithmetic Rate Problem**

(1) Given that Maria drove 60 miles before overtaking her husband, it is not possible to determine how many hours she spent in driving this distance. For example, she could have been driving this distance at a rate of 30 miles per hour, and thus spent 2 hours in driving this distance. However, she could also have been driving this distance at a rate of 60 miles per hour, and thus spent 1 hour in driving this distance; NOT sufficient.

(2) Given that Maria drove at an average of 60 miles per hour and her husband drove at an average of 60 − 12 = 48 miles per hour, and letting $t$ be the number of hours it took for Maria to overtake her husband, it follows that $60t = 48(t + \frac{1}{4})$ since the distance Maria drove, $60t$ miles, is the same as the distance her husband drove, $48(t + \frac{1}{4})$ miles. Therefore, $60t = 48t + 12$, or $t = 1$, and hence it took 1 hour for Maria to overtake her husband; SUFFICIENT.

**The correct answer is B;
statement 2 alone is sufficient.**

12. In a school that had a total of 600 students enrolled in the junior and senior classes, the students contributed to a certain fund. If all of the juniors but only half of the seniors contributed, was the total amount contributed more than $740 ?

(1) Each junior contributed $1 and each senior who contributed gave $3.

(2) There were more juniors than seniors enrolled in the school.

**Arithmetic Applied Problems**

The task in this question is to determine whether the respective statements are sufficient for answering the question of whether the total amount contributed was more than $740. In making this determination, it is important to remember that we are to use only the information that has been given. For example, it may seem plausible to assume that the number of seniors at the school is roughly equal to the number of juniors. However, because no such information has been provided, we cannot assume that this assumption holds. With this in mind, consider statements 1 and 2.

(1) If it were the case that half of the 600 students were seniors, then, given that half of the 300 seniors would have contributed $3, there would have been $150 \times \$3 = \$450$ in contributions from the seniors and $300 \times \$1 = \$300$ in contributions from the juniors, for a total of $750—more than the figure of $740 with which the question is concerned. However, as noted, we cannot make such an assumption. To test the conditions that we have actually been given, we can consider extreme cases, which are often relatively simple. For example, given the information provided, it is possible that only two of the students are seniors and the other 598 students are juniors. If this were the case, then the contributions from the juniors would be $598 ($1 per student) and the contributions from the seniors would be $3 ($3 for the one senior who contributes, given that only half of the 2 seniors contribute). The total contributions would then be $598 + $3 = $601; NOT sufficient.

(2)  Merely with this statement—and not statement 1—we have no information as to how much the students contributed. We therefore cannot determine the total amount contributed; NOT sufficient.

We still need to consider whether statements 1 and 2 are sufficient *together* for determining whether a minimum of $740 has been contributed. However, note that the reasoning in connection with statement 1 applies here as well. We considered there the possibility that the 600 students included only two seniors, with the other 598 students being juniors. Because this scenario also satisfies statement 2, we see that statements 1 and 2 taken together are not sufficient.

**The correct answer is E;
both statements together are still not sufficient.**

13. How much did credit-card fraud cost United States banks in year X to the nearest $10 million?

   (1)  In year X, counterfeit cards and telephone and mail-order fraud accounted for 39 percent of the total amount that card fraud cost the banks.

   (2)  In year X, stolen cards accounted for $158.4 million, or 16 percent, of the total amount that credit-card fraud cost the banks.

**Arithmetic** Percents

   (1)  It is given that certain parts of the total fraud cost have a total that is 39% of the total fraud cost, but since no actual dollar amounts are specified, it is not possible to estimate the total fraud cost to the nearest $10 million; NOT sufficient.

   (2)  Given that $158.4 million represents 16% of the total fraud cost, it follows that the total fraud cost equals $158.4 million divided by 0.16; SUFFICIENT.

**The correct answer is B;
statement 2 alone is sufficient.**

14. Company X's profits this year increased by 25% over last year's profits. Was the dollar amount of Company X's profits this year greater than the dollar amount of Company Y's?

   (1)  Last year, the ratio of Company Y's profits to Company X's profits was 5:2.

   (2)  Company Y experienced a 40% drop in profits from last year to this year.

**Algebra** Applied Problems

Let $P_X$ and $P_X'$, respectively, be the profits of Company X last year and this year, and let $P_Y$ and $P_Y'$, respectively, be the profits of Company Y last year and this year. Then $P_X' = 1.25P_X$. Is $P_X' > P_Y'$ ?

   (1)  Given that $\dfrac{P_Y}{P_X} = \dfrac{5}{2}$, it is not possible to determine whether $P_X' > P_Y'$ because nothing is known about the value of $P_Y'$ other than $P_Y'$ is positive; NOT sufficient.

   (2)  Given that $P_Y' = 0.6P_Y$, it is not possible to determine whether $P_X' > P_Y'$ because nothing is known that relates the profits of Company X for either year to the profits of Company Y for either year; NOT sufficient.

Taking (1) and (2) together, it is given that $P_X' = 1.25P_X$ and from (1) it follows that $\dfrac{P_Y}{P_X} = \dfrac{5}{2}$, or $P_X = \dfrac{2}{5}P_Y$, and thus $P_X' = (1.25)\left(\dfrac{2}{5}P_Y\right)$. From (2) it follows that $P_Y' = 0.6P_Y$, or $P_Y = \dfrac{1}{0.6}P_Y'$, and thus $P_X' = (1.25)\left(\dfrac{2}{5}\right)\left(\dfrac{1}{0.6}P_Y'\right)$. Since the last equation expresses $P_X'$ as a specific number times $P_Y'$, it follows that it can be determined whether or not $P_X' > P_Y'$. Note that $(1.25)\left(\dfrac{2}{5}\right)\left(\dfrac{1}{0.6}\right) = \left(\dfrac{5}{4}\right)\left(\dfrac{2}{5}\right)\left(\dfrac{5}{3}\right) = \dfrac{5}{6}$, and so the answer to the question "Is $P_X' > P_Y'$" is no.

**The correct answer is C;
both statements together are sufficient.**

15. A certain company consists of three divisions, A, B, and C. Of the employees in the three divisions, the employees in Division C have the greatest average (arithmetic mean) annual salary. Is the average annual salary of the employees in the three divisions combined less than $55,000 ?

   (1)  The average annual salary of the employees in Divisions A and B combined is $45,000.

   (2)  The average annual salary of the employees in Division C is $55,000.

**Algebra** Statistics

(1)   Given that the average annual salary of the employees in Divisions A and B combined is $45,000, each of the divisions could have exactly two employees such that the annual salaries in Division A are $45,000 and $45,000, the annual salaries in Division B are $45,000 and $45,000, and the annual salaries in Division C are $50,000 and $50,000, in which case Division C has the greatest average annual salary and the average annual salary in Divisions A, B, and C combined is less than $55,000. On the other hand, each of the divisions could have exactly two employees such that the annual salaries in Division A are $45,000 and $45,000, the annual salaries in Division B are $45,000 and $45,000, and the annual salaries in Division C are $1 million and $1 million, in which case Division C has the greatest average annual salary and the average annual salary in Divisions A, B, and C combined is greater than $55,000; NOT sufficient.

(2)   Given that the average annual salary in Division C is $55,000, we have $\frac{\Sigma_C}{N_C} = 55,000$, where $\Sigma_C$ is the sum of the annual salaries, in dollars, of the employees in Division C and $N_C$ is the number of employees in Division C. Moreover, letting $\Sigma_A$ and $\Sigma_B$ be the sums of the annual salaries, respectively and in dollars, of the employees in Divisions A and B, and letting $N_A$ and $N_B$ be the numbers of employees, respectively, in Divisions A and B, then we have $\frac{\Sigma_A}{N_A} < 55,000$ and $\frac{\Sigma_B}{N_B} < 55,000$, since the employees in Division C have the greatest average annual salary. Note that these two inequalities and this equation can be rewritten as $\Sigma_A < 55,000N_A$, $\Sigma_B < 55,000N_B$, and $\Sigma_C = 55,000N_C$. Therefore, the average annual salary of the employees in the three divisions combined is $\frac{\Sigma_A + \Sigma_B + \Sigma_C}{N_A + N_B + N_C} =$

$\frac{\Sigma_A + \Sigma_B + 55,000N_C}{N_A + N_B + N_C}$, which is less than

$\frac{55,000N_A + 55,000N_B + 55,000N_C}{N_A + N_B + N_C} =$

$\frac{55,000(N_A + N_B + N_C)}{N_A + N_B + N_C} = 55,000;$ SUFFICIENT.

**The correct answer is B; statement 2 alone is sufficient.**

16.   A candle company determines that, for a certain specialty candle, the supply function is $p = m_1x + b_1$ and the demand function is $p = m_2x + b_2$, where $p$ is the price of each candle, $x$ is the number of candles supplied or demanded, and $m_1$, $m_2$, $b_1$, and $b_2$ are constants. At what value of $x$ do the graphs of the supply function and demand function intersect?

(1)   $m_1 = -m_2 = 0.005$
(2)   $b_2 - b_1 = 6$

**Algebra** First-Degree Equations

The graphs will intersect at the value of $x$ such that $m_1x + b_1 = m_2x + b_2$ or $(m_1 - m_2)x = b_2 - b_1$.

(1)   This indicates that $m_1 = -m_2 = 0.005$. It follows that $m_1 - m_2 = 0.01$, and so $0.01x = b_2 - b_1$ or $x = 100(b_2 - b_1)$, which can vary as the values of $b_2$ and $b_1$ vary; NOT sufficient.

(2)   This indicates that $b_2 - b_1 = 6$. It follows that $(m_1 - m_2)x = 6$. This implies that $m_1 \neq m_2$, and so $x = \frac{b_2 - b_1}{m_1 - m_2} = \frac{6}{m_1 - m_2}$, which can vary as the values of $m_1$ and $m_2$ vary; NOT sufficient.

Taking (1) and (2) together, $m_1 - m_2 = 0.01$ and $b_2 - b_1 = 6$ and so the value of $x$ is $\frac{6}{0.01} = 600$.

**The correct answer is C; both statements together are sufficient.**

17.   A certain ski shop sold 125 pairs of skis and 100 pairs of ski boots for a total of $75,000. What was the average (arithmetic mean) selling price of a pair of the ski boots?

(1)   The average selling price of a pair of skis was $300.
(2)   The selling price of a pair of ski boots varied from $150 to $900.

**Arithmetic** Statistics

Let $\Sigma_{skis}$ be the sum of the selling prices, in dollars, of all 125 pairs of skis and let $\Sigma_{boots}$ be the sum of the selling prices, in dollars, of all 100 pairs of ski boots. We are given that $\Sigma_{skis} + \Sigma_{boots} = 75{,}000$. Determine the value of $\dfrac{\Sigma_{boots}}{100}$, or equivalently, determine the value of $\Sigma_{boots}$.

(1) Given that $\dfrac{\Sigma_{skis}}{125} = 300$, or $\Sigma_{skis} = 300(125) = 37{,}500$, it follows from $\Sigma_{skis} + \Sigma_{boots} = 75{,}000$ that $\Sigma_{boots} = 75{,}000 - \Sigma_{skis} = 75{,}000 - 37{,}500 = 37{,}500$; SUFFICIENT.

(2) Given that the selling price of a pair of ski boots varied from \$150 to \$900, it is possible that there were 40 pairs of ski boots each with a selling price of \$150, 60 pairs of ski boots each with a selling price of \$900, and 125 pairs of skis each with a selling price of \$120 for a total selling price of $40(\$150) + 60(\$900) + 125(\$120) = \$75{,}000$, and thus it is possible that $\Sigma_{boots} = 40(150) + 60(900) = 6{,}000 + 54{,}000 = 60{,}000$. However, it is also possible that there were 60 pairs of ski boots each with a selling price of \$150, 40 pairs of ski boots each with a selling price of \$900, and 125 pairs of skis each with a selling price of \$240 for a total selling price of $60(\$150) + 40(\$900) + 125(\$240) = \$75{,}000$, and thus it is also possible that $\Sigma_{boots} = 60(150) + 40(900) = 9{,}000 + 36{,}000 = 45{,}000$; NOT sufficient.

**The correct answer is A; statement 1 alone is sufficient.**

18. Last year Publisher X published 1,100 books, consisting of first editions, revised editions, and reprints. How many first editions did Publisher X publish last year?

    (1) The number of first editions published was 50 more than twice the number of reprints published.

    (2) The number of revised editions published was half the number of reprints published.

**Algebra** Simultaneous Equations

Let $A$ be the number of first editions, $B$ be the number of revised editions, and $C$ be the number of reprints. Then $A + B + C = 1{,}100$. Determine the value of $A$.

(1) Given that $A = 50 + 2C$, it is not possible to determine the value of $A$. This is because by choosing different values of $C$, different values of $A$ can be obtained by using the equation $A = 50 + 2C$, and then the equation $A + B + C = 1{,}100$ can be used to determine whether acceptable values of $B$ (nonnegative integers) exist for these values of $A$ and $C$. For example, choosing $C = 100$ leads to $A = 250$ and $B = 750$, and choosing $C = 200$ leads to $A = 450$ and $B = 450$; NOT sufficient.

(2) Given that $B = \dfrac{1}{2}C$, or $C = 2B$, it is not possible to determine the value of $A$. This is because by choosing different values of $B$, different values of $C$ can be obtained by using the equation $C = 2B$, and then the equation $A + B + C = 1{,}100$ can be used to determine different values of $A$. For example, choosing $B = 100$ leads to $C = 200$ and $A = 800$, and choosing $B = 200$ leads to $C = 400$ and $A = 500$; NOT sufficient.

Taking $A = 50 + 2C$ from (1) and $C = 2B$ from (2) together gives $A = 50 + 4B$. Thus, in the equation $A + B + C = 1{,}100$, $A$ can be replaced with $50 + 4B$ and $C$ can be replaced with $2B$ to give $(50 + 4B) + B + 2B = 1{,}100$. Solving for $B$ gives $B = 150$, and hence $C = 2B = 300$ and $A = 50 + 2C = 650$.

**The correct answer is C; both statements together are sufficient.**

19. How old is Jane?

    (1) Ten years ago she was one-third as old as she is now.

    (2) In 15 years, she will be twice as old as she is now.

**Algebra** First-Degree Equations

Determine the value of $J$, where $J$ represents Jane's current age.

(1) In symbols, $J - 10$ represents Jane's age ten years ago and $\dfrac{1}{3}J$ represents one-third her current age. These expressions are equal by

(1), so $J - 10 = \frac{1}{3}J$. This is a first-degree equation in the variable $J$ and has a unique solution; SUFFICIENT.

(2)  In symbols, $J + 15$ represents Jane's age 15 years from now and $2J$ represents twice her current age. These expressions are equal by (2), so $J + 15 = 2J$. This is a first-degree equation in the variable $J$ and has a unique solution; SUFFICIENT.

**The correct answer is D; each statement alone is sufficient.**

20.  What was the population of City X in 2002 ?

(1)  X's population in 2002 increased by 2 percent, or 20,000 people, over 2001.

(2)  In 2001, X's population was 1,000,000.

**Algebra Percents**

Letting $P_1$ and $P_2$ represent City X's population in 2001 and 2002, respectively, the percent increase in population from 2001 to 2002 is given as a decimal by $\frac{P_2 - P_1}{P_1}$.

(1)  By (1) the percent increase was 2 percent, so $\frac{P_2 - P_1}{P_1} = 0.02$ or $P_2 - P_1 = 0.02P_1$. Also, by (1), $P_2 - P_1 = 20,000$, so $20,000 = 0.02P_1$ from which the value of $P_1$ can be uniquely determined. Then $P_1 + 20,000 = P_2$, which is the population of City X in 2002; SUFFICIENT.

(2)  Even though (2) gives $P_1 = 1,000,000$, it gives no information about the population of City X in 2002 either by itself or in relation to the population in 2001; NOT sufficient.

**The correct answer is A; statement 1 alone is sufficient.**

21.  Yesterday Bookstore B sold twice as many softcover books as hardcover books. Was Bookstore B's revenue from the sale of softcover books yesterday greater than its revenue from the sale of hardcover books yesterday?

(1)  The average (arithmetic mean) price of the hardcover books sold at the store yesterday was $10 more than the average price of the softcover books sold at the store yesterday.

(2)  The average price of the softcover and hardcover books sold at the store yesterday was greater than $14.

**Arithmetic Statistics**

Letting $s$ represent the number of softcover books sold; $h$, the number of hardcover books sold; $S$, the average price of the softcover books sold; and $H$, the average price of the hardcover books sold, determine whether the revenue from the sale of softcover books is greater than the revenue from the sale of hardcover books or if $sS > hH$, where $s = 2h$.

(1)  Given that $H = S + 10$, if $S = 10$, $H = 20$, $s = 10$, and $h = 5$, then $sS = 100$ and $hH = 100$, so $sS = hH$. On the other hand, if $S = 40$, $H = 50$, $s = 8$, and $h - 4$, then $sS = 320$ and $hH = 200$, so $sS > hH$; NOT sufficient.

(2)  Given that $\frac{sS + hH}{s + h} > 14$, if $s = 6$, $S = 10$, $h = 3$, and $H = 30$, $\frac{6(10) + 3(30)}{6 + 3} = \frac{150}{9} > 14$ and $6(10) < 3(30)$. On the other hand, if $s = 10$, $S = 15$, $h = 5$, and $H = 20$, $\frac{10(15) + 5(20)}{10 + 5} = \frac{250}{15} > 14$ and $10(15) > 5(20)$; NOT sufficient.

Taking (1) and (2) together,

| | | | |
|---|---|---|---|
| $\frac{sS + hH}{s + h}$ | $>$ | $14$ | from (2) |
| $\frac{2h(H - 10) + hH}{2h + h}$ | $>$ | $14$ | $s = 2h$ (given) and $H = S + 10$ from (1) |
| $\frac{3H - 20}{3}$ | $>$ | $14$ | cancel $h$ and simplify |
| $3H - 20$ | $>$ | $42$ | multiply both sides by 3 |
| $H$ | $>$ | $\frac{62}{3}$ | solve for $H$ |

To show that this leads to $sS > hH$, start with $sS > hH$ and then reverse the steps.

| $sS$ | $>$ | $hH$ | |
|---|---|---|---|
| $2h(H-10)$ | $>$ | $hH$ | $s = 2h$ and $S = H - 10$ |
| $2hH - 20h$ | $>$ | $hH$ | distributive property |
| $2hH$ | $>$ | $hH + 20h$ | add $20h$ to both sides |
| $hH$ | $>$ | $20h$ | subtract $hH$ from both sides |
| $H$ | $>$ | $20$ | divide both sides by $h > 0$ |

Now, reverse the steps.

| $H$ | $>$ | $\dfrac{62}{3}$ | derived earlier |
|---|---|---|---|
| $H$ | $>$ | $20$ | $\dfrac{62}{3} > 20$ |
| $hH$ | $>$ | $20h$ | multiply both sides by $h > 0$ |
| $2hH$ | $>$ | $hH + 20h$ | add $hH$ to both sides |
| $2hH - 20h$ | $>$ | $hH$ | subtract $20h$ from both sides |
| $2h(H-10)$ | $>$ | $hH$ | factor |
| $sS$ | $>$ | $hH$ | $s = 2h$ and $S = H - 10$ |

Thus, the revenue from the sale of softcover books was greater than the revenue from the sale of hardcover books.

**The correct answer is C;
both statements together are sufficient.**

22. A customer purchased 6 shirts priced at $10.99 each, excluding sales tax. How much sales tax did he pay on this purchase?

    (1) The customer paid a 5 percent sales tax on the total price of the shirts.

    (2) The customer paid a total of $11.54 for each shirt, including sales tax.

**Arithmetic Percents**

Determine the sales tax paid by a customer who bought six shirts for $10.99 each, excluding sales tax.

(1) Given that the sales tax was 5%, the customer paid sales tax totaling $3.30, which is 6(0.05)($10.99), rounded to the nearest cent; SUFFICIENT.

(2) Given that each shirt cost $11.54 including sales tax, the customer paid a total of 6($11.54 – $10.99) = $3.30 in sales tax; SUFFICIENT.

**The correct answer is D;
each statement alone is sufficient.**

23. The sum of the lengths of two pieces of rope is 65 feet. How long is the shorter piece?

    (1) The lengths of the pieces of rope are in the ratio 8 : 5.

    (2) One piece of rope is 15 feet longer than the other piece.

**Algebra Ratio and Proportion; First-Degree Equations**

The sum of the lengths of two pieces of rope is 65 feet. Determine the length of the shorter piece of rope.

(1) Given that the lengths of the pieces of rope are in the ratio 8:5, it follows that $8x + 5x = 65$, for some value of $x$. Hence, $13x = 65$ and $x = 5$. The length of the shorter piece is $5(5) = 25$; SUFFICIENT.

(2) Given that one piece is 15 feet longer than the other piece, if $s$ represents the length of the shorter piece, it follows that $s + (s + 15) = 65$, $2s + 15 = 65$, $2s = 50$, and $s = 25$; SUFFICIENT.

**The correct answer is D;
each statement alone is sufficient.**

24. An initial investment of $10,000 was deposited in a bank account one year ago, and additional deposits were made during the year. If no withdrawals were made, what was the total amount of interest earned on this account during the year?

    (1) The additional deposits during the year totaled

    (2) The account earned interest at the annual rate of 6 percent compounded quarterly.

**Arithmetic** Applied Problems

Determine the interest earned in one year by an initial investment of $10,000 with additional deposits, but no withdrawals, during the year.

(1)  Given that the additional deposits total $5,000, it is not possible to determine the interest earned by both the initial investment and the additional deposits together without information about the interest rate and when during the year the additional deposits were made; NOT sufficient.

(2)  Given that the annual interest rate is 6% compounded quarterly, it is not possible to determine the interest earned by both the initial investment and the additional deposits together without information about the amount of the additional deposits and when during the year the additional deposits were made; NOT sufficient.

Taking (1) and (2) together, it is not possible to determine the interest earned by both the initial investment and the additional deposits together without information about when during the year the additional deposits were made. For example, if one deposit of $5,000 were made after 6 months, then the interest for the year would be more than it would have been had the $5,000 been deposited after 9 months.

**The correct answer is E;**
**both statements together are still not sufficient.**

25.  A poplar tree was 3 feet high when it was planted on January 1, 1970. During what year did it pass the height of 20 feet?

(1)  On January 1, 1973, it was 24 feet high.
(2)  It doubled its height during each year.

**Arithmetic** Series and Sequences

(1)  Given that the tree was 24 feet high at the beginning of 1973, it is not possible to determine during which year the tree passed the height of 20 feet.

| year | beginning height (ft) | ending height (ft) | feet grown (ft) |
|------|----------------------|-------------------|-----------------|
| 1970 | 3 | 15 | 12 |
| 1971 | 15 | 21 | 6 |
| 1972 | 21 | 24 | 3 |
| 1973 | 24 | 30 | 6 |

| year | beginning height (ft) | ending height (ft) | feet grown (ft) |
|------|----------------------|-------------------|-----------------|
| 1970 | 3 | 6 | 3 |
| 1971 | 6 | 12 | 6 |
| 1972 | 12 | 24 | 12 |
| 1973 | 24 | 30 | 6 |

The first table shows that the tree could have passed the height of 20 feet during 1971 and the second table shows that the tree could have passed the height of 20 feet during 1972; NOT sufficient.

(2)  Given that the tree doubled its height during each year, the tree would have been 6 feet high at the beginning of 1971, 12 feet high at the beginning of 1972, and 24 feet high at the beginning of 1973. Therefore, the tree would have passed the height of 20 feet during 1972; SUFFICIENT.

**The correct answer is B;**
**statement 2 alone is sufficient.**

26.  Which weighs more, a cubic unit of water or a cubic unit of liquid X ?

(1)  A cubic unit of water weighs more than $\frac{1}{3}$ cubic unit of liquid X.

(2)  A cubic unit of liquid X weighs less than 3 cubic units of water.

**Algebra** Inequalities

Determine which is greater: the weight of a cubic unit of water, represented by $W$, or a cubic unit of Liquid X, represented by $X$.

(1) Given that $W > \frac{1}{3}X$, it is not possible to determine which of $W$ and $X$ is greater. For example, if $W = 4$ and $X = 9$, then $W > \frac{1}{3}X$ and $X$ is greater than $W$, but if $W = 10$ and $X = 9$, then $W > \frac{1}{3}X$ and $W$ is greater than $X$; NOT sufficient.

(2) Given that $X < 3W$, it is not possible to determine which of $W$ and $X$ is greater. For example, if $X = 9$ and $W = 4$, then $X < 3W$ and $X$ is greater than $W$, but if $X = 9$ and $W = 10$, then $X < 3W$ and $W$ is greater than $X$; NOT sufficient.

Taking (1) and (2) together gives no more information than (1) or (2) alone since the same examples used to show that (1) is not sufficient also show that (2) is not sufficient.

**The correct answer is E;
both statements together are still not sufficient.**

27. What were the individual prices of the vases that an antique dealer bought at store X ?

(1) The antique dealer bought exactly 3 vases at store X.
(2) The antique dealer's total bill at store X was $225.

**Arithmetic Applied Problems**

Determine the individual prices of the vases.

(1) Given that there are 3 vases, it is not possible to determine the individual prices because no information about prices is known or can be determined; NOT sufficient.

(2) Given that the total bill was $225, it is not possible to determine the individual prices because neither the number of vases nor whether the vases are identically or otherwise priced is known or can be determined; NOT sufficient.

Taking (1) and (2) together, it is still not possible to determine the individual prices of the vases. For example, the prices of the 3 vases could be $200, $20, and $5 for a total bill of $225. However, the prices of the 3 vases could also be $100, $100, and $25 for a total bill of $225.

**The correct answer is E;
both statements together are still not sufficient.**

28. Was the average (arithmetic mean) sale price of a new home in region R last month at least $100,000?

(1) Last month the median sale price of a new home in region R was at least $100,000.
(2) Last month the sale prices of new homes in region R ranged from $75,000 to $150,000.

**Arithmetic Statistics**

(1) Given that the median price was at least $100,000, the following two examples show that it cannot be determined whether the average price was at least $100,000.

Example 1: Average price is greater than $100,000

| $75,000 | **$100,000** | $150,000 |
|---------|--------------|----------|
| $100,000 | | $150,000 |
| $100,000 | | $150,000 |

The median of these 7 prices is $100,000 and the average of these prices is greater than $100,000, since the sum of these 7 prices is $7(\$100,000) + (-\$25,000 + \$50,000 + \$50,000 + \$50,000)$, which is greater than $7(\$100,000)$.

Example 2: Average price is less than $100,000

| $75,000 | **$100,000** | $150,000 |
|---------|--------------|----------|
| $100,000 | | $150,000 |
| $100,000 | | $150,000 |

The median of these 7 prices is $100,000 and the average of these prices is less than $100,000, since the sum of these 7 prices is $7(\$100,000) + (-\$25,000 - \$25,000 - \$25,000 + \$50,000)$, which is less than $7(\$100,000)$; NOT sufficient.

(2) Given that the prices ranged from $75,000 to $150,000, the same examples above show that it cannot be determined whether the average price was at least $100,000; NOT sufficient.

Taking (1) and (2) together, it cannot be determined whether the average price was at least $100,000 because the two examples above each satisfy both (1) and (2).

**The correct answer is E;
both statements together are still not sufficient.**

29. If the capacity of tank X is less than the capacity of tank Y and both tanks begin to fill at the same time, which tank will be filled first?

    (1) Tank X is filled at a constant rate of 1.5 liters per minute.

    (2) Tank Y is filled at a constant rate of 120 liters per hour.

**Arithmetic Applied Problems**

Determine which tank, X or Y, will be filled first if X has less capacity than Y and they start filling at the same time.

(1) Given that X fills at a rate of 1.5 liters per minute, which is equivalent to 90 liters per hour, it is not possible to determine which tank will be filled first because no information is given about the rate at which Y fills or about how much larger in capacity Y is than X; NOT sufficient.

(2) Given that Y fills at a rate of 120 liters per hour, it is not possible to determine which tank will be filled first because no information is given about the rate at which X fills or about how much larger in capacity Y is than X; NOT sufficient.

Taking (1) and (2) together, if the capacity of X is 90 liters and the capacity of Y is 200 liters, then X will be filled in 1 hour but Y will be only 60% filled in 1 hour. Therefore, X will be filled first. On the other hand, if the capacity of X is 90 liters and the capacity of Y is 100 liters, then Y will be filled in $\frac{5}{6}$ hours while X will take a full hour to be filled. Thus, Y will be filled first.

**The correct answer is E; both statements together are still not sufficient.**

30. At a certain company, 30 percent of the employees live in City R. If 25 percent of the company's employees live in apartments in City R, what is the number of the employees who live in apartments in City R?

    (1) Of the employees who live in City R, 6 do <u>not</u> live in apartments.

    (2) Of the employees, 84 do <u>not</u> live in City R.

**Arithmetic Percents**

Determine how many employees of a certain company live in apartments in City R, where 30% of the employees live in City R and 25% of the employees live in apartments in City R. Let T represent the total number of employees at the company.

(1) Given that 6 of the employees who live in City R do not live in apartments, it follows that $6 = (0.30 - 0.25)T$. Thus $0.05T = 6$, $T = 120$, and the number of employees who live in apartments in City R can be determined; SUFFICIENT.

(2) Given that 84 employees do not live in City R, it follows that $(1 - 0.3)T = 84$, from which it follows that $T = 120$ and the number of employees who live in apartments in City R can be determined; SUFFICIENT.

**The correct answer is D; each statement alone is sufficient.**

31. What was Mary's average (arithmetic mean) score on 4 tests?

    (1) Her average (arithmetic mean) score on 3 of the tests was 97.

    (2) Her score on one of the tests was 96.

**Arithmetic Statistics**

Since the average of the 4 scores is equal to the sum of the 4 scores divided by 4, it follows that the average of the 4 scores can be determined if and only if the sum of the 4 scores can be determined.

(1) Given that the sum of 3 of the scores was 3(97), it is not possible to determine the sum of the 4 scores, since different values for the remaining score are possible and those different values correspond to different values for the sum of the 4 scores; NOT sufficient.

(2) Given that one of the scores was 96, it is not possible to determine the sum of the 4 scores, since different values for the sum of the remaining 3 scores are possible and those different values correspond to different values for the sum of the 4 scores; NOT sufficient.

Taking (1) and (2) together, it is still not possible to determine the sum of the 4 scores. For example, the scores could be 96, 97, 98, 10 (the first 3 listed scores have an average of 97 and one of the scores is 96), which have an average that is less than 96, and the scores could be 96, 97, 98, 99 (the first 3 listed scores have an average of 97 and one of the scores is 96), which have an average that is greater than 96.

**The correct answer is E; both statements together are still not sufficient.**

## Questions 32 to 59 - Difficulty: **Medium**

32. The table shows the number of people who responded "yes" or "no" or "don't know" when asked whether their city council should implement environmental programs X and Y. If a total of 1,000 people responded to the question about both programs, what was the number of people who did not respond "yes" to implementing either of the two programs?

    (1) The number of people who responded "yes" to implementing only Program X was 300.

    (2) The number of people who responded "no" to implementing Program X and "no" to implementing Program Y was 100.

    **Arithmetic** Interpretation of Tables; Sets (Venn Diagrams)

    (1) Given that 300 people responded "yes" to implementing only Program X, and because 400 people altogether responded "yes" to implementing Program X, it follows that 400 − 300 = 100 people responded "yes" to implementing both Program X and Program Y. Therefore, because 300 people altogether responded "yes" to implementing Program Y, 300 − 100 = 200 people responded "yes" to implementing only Program Y. These results are shown in the Venn diagram below.

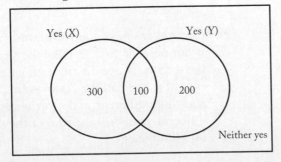

Since the Venn diagram above represents a total of 1,000 people, it follows that the number of people who did not respond "yes" to implementing either Program X or Program Y is 1,000 − (300 + 100 + 200) = 400; SUFFICIENT.

(2) Given that 100 people responded "no" both to implementing Program X and to implementing Program Y, the table below shows a possibility whereby the number of people who did not respond "yes" to implementing either Program X or Program Y could be 400. Note that for each of the column headings "Yes," "No," and "Don't Know," the numbers under that column heading satisfy (X answered) + (Y answered) − (both answered) + (neither answered) = 1,000. Indeed, for each of these three columns a Venn diagram can be given that represents the numbers in that column.

|         | Yes   | No    | Don't Know |
|---------|-------|-------|------------|
| X       | 400   | 200   | 400        |
| Y       | 300   | 350   | 350        |
| Both    | 100   | 100   | 0          |
| Neither | **400** | 550 | 250        |
| Total   | 1,000 | 1,000 | 1,000      |

However, the next table shows a possibility whereby the number of people who did not respond "yes" to implementing either Program X or Program Y could be 500.

|         | Yes   | No    | Don't Know |
|---------|-------|-------|------------|
| X       | 400   | 200   | 400        |
| Y       | 300   | 350   | 350        |
| Both    | 200   | 100   | 0          |
| Neither | **500** | 550 | 250        |
| Total   | 1,000 | 1,000 | 1,000      |

Therefore, among other possibilities, the number of people who did not respond "yes" to implementing either Program X or Program Y could be 400, and this number could also be 500; NOT sufficient.

**The correct answer is A; statement 1 alone is sufficient.**

33. An estimate of an actual data value has an error of $p$ percent if $p = \dfrac{100|e-a|}{a}$, where $e$ is the estimated value and $a$ is the actual value. Emma's estimate for her total income last year had an error of less than 20 percent. Emma's estimate of her income from tutoring last year also had an error of less than 20 percent. Was Emma's actual income from tutoring last year at most 45 percent of her actual total income last year?

    (1) Emma's estimated income last year from tutoring was 30 percent of her estimated total income last year.

    (2) Emma's estimated total income last year was $40,000.

### Arithmetic Estimation

Given that Emma's estimates for both her total income and her income from tutoring last year, $E_I$ and $E_T$, respectively, were within 20 percent of her actual total income and her actual income from tutoring, $A_I$ and $A_T$, respectively, it follows that $0.8E_I < A_I < 1.2E_I$ and $0.8E_T < A_T < 1.2E_T$.

Determine whether Emma's actual income from tutoring was at most 45 percent of her actual total income or if $\dfrac{A_T}{A_I} \leq 0.45$.

    (1) Given that $E_T = 0.3E_I$, it follows from $0.8E_T < A_T < 1.2E_T$ that $0.24E_I < A_T < 0.36E_I$. Then, since $0.8E_I < A_I < 1.2E_I$, it follows that

    $\dfrac{1}{1.2E_I} < \dfrac{1}{A_I} < \dfrac{1}{0.8E_I}$. Multiplying the

    inequalities gives $\dfrac{0.24E_I}{1.2E_I} < \dfrac{A_T}{A_I} < \dfrac{0.36E_I}{0.8E_I}$

    or $0.2 < \dfrac{A_T}{A_I} < 0.45$; SUFFICIENT.

    (2) Given that Emma's estimated total income last year was $40,000, it is impossible to determine whether her actual income from tutoring was at most 45 percent of her actual total income because no information is given about her actual income from tutoring other than it was within 20 percent of her estimated income from tutoring. And there is no information from which her estimated income from tutoring can be determined; NOT sufficient.

**The correct answer is A;
statement 1 alone is sufficient.**

34. Was Store K's profit last month at least 10 percent greater than its profit the previous month?

    (1) Store K's expenses last month were 5 percent greater than its expenses the previous month.

    (2) Store K's revenues last month were 10 percent greater than its revenues the previous month.

### Algebra Applied Problems

Let $P_{last}$, $E_{last}$, and $R_{last}$ be, respectively, the profit, expenses, and revenues for last month. Also, let $P_{previous}$, $E_{previous}$, and $R_{previous}$ be, respectively, the profit, expenses, and revenues for the previous month. Then we have $P_{last} = R_{last} - E_{last}$ and $P_{previous} = R_{previous} - E_{previous}$. Determine whether $P_{last} \geq 1.1P_{previous}$ is true, or equivalently, determine whether $R_{last} - E_{last} \geq 1.1R_{previous} - 1.1E_{previous}$ is true.

    (1) Given that $E_{last} = 1.05E_{previous}$, it follows that the inequality $R_{last} - E_{last} \geq 1.1R_{previous} - 1.1E_{previous}$ is equivalent to $R_{last} - 1.1R_{previous} \geq -0.05E_{previous}$. It is clear that, for suitable values of $R_{last}$, $R_{previous}$, and $E_{previous}$, this last inequality could be true and this last inequality could be false; NOT sufficient.

    (2) Given that $R_{last} = 1.1R_{previous}$, it follows that the inequality $R_{last} - E_{last} \geq 1.1R_{previous} - 1.1E_{previous}$ is equivalent to $E_{last} \leq 1.1E_{previous}$. It is clear that, for suitable values of $E_{last}$ and $E_{previous}$, this last inequality could be true and this last inequality could be false; NOT sufficient.

Taking (1) and (2) together, the following shows that $P_{last} \geq 1.1P_{previous}$ is true.

$$\begin{aligned} P_{last} &= R_{last} - E_{last} \\ &= 1.1R_{previous} - 1.05E_{previous} \\ &\geq 1.1R_{previous} - 1.1E_{previous} \end{aligned}$$

Therefore, $P_{last} \geq 1.1(R_{previous} - E_{previous})$, and hence $P_{last} \geq 1.1P_{previous}$ is true. (The reason for using $\geq$ above instead of $>$ is to allow for the possibility that $E_{previous} = 0$.)

**The correct answer is C;
both statements together are sufficient.**

35. Gross profit is equal to selling price minus cost. A car dealer's gross profit on the sale of a certain car was what percent of the cost of the car?

    (1) The selling price of the car was $\frac{11}{10}$ of the cost of the car.

    (2) The cost of the car was $14,500.

### Arithmetic Applied Problems

Determine the gross profit, $P$, on the sale of a car as a percent of the cost, $C$, of the car.

(1) Given that the selling price of the car was $\frac{11}{10}C$, $P = \frac{11}{10}C - C = \frac{1}{10}C$. Thus, the profit was 10% of the cost of the car; SUFFICIENT.

(2) Given that the cost of the car was $14,500, it is impossible to determine the profit because the selling price is not known nor is there enough information to determine it; NOT sufficient.

**The correct answer is A; statement 1 alone is sufficient.**

36. When the wind speed is 9 miles per hour, the wind-chill factor $w$ is given by

$$w = -17.366 + 1.19t,$$

where $t$ is the temperature in degrees Fahrenheit. If at noon yesterday the wind speed was 9 miles per hour, was the wind-chill factor greater than 0 ?

    (1) The temperature at noon yesterday was greater than 10 degrees Fahrenheit.

    (2) The temperature at noon yesterday was less than 20 degrees Fahrenheit.

### Algebra Applied Problems

Determine whether $-17.366 + 1.19t$ is greater than 0.

(1) Given that $t > 10$, it follows that $-17.366 + 1.19t > -17.366 + 1.19(10)$, or $-17.366 + 1.19t > -5.466$. However, it is not possible to determine whether $-17.366 + 1.19t$ is greater than 0. For example, if $t = 19$, then $-17.366 + 1.19t = 5.244$ is greater than 0. However, if $t = 11$, then $-17.366 + 1.19t = -4.276$, which is not greater than 0; NOT sufficient.

(2) Given that $t < 20$, the same examples used in (1) show that it is not possible to determine whether $-17.366 + 1.19t$ is greater than 0; NOT sufficient.

Taking (1) and (2) together is of no more help than either (1) or (2) taken separately because the same examples were used in both (1) and (2).

**The correct answer is E; both statements together are still not sufficient.**

37. How many members of a certain legislature voted against the measure to raise their salaries?

    (1) $\frac{1}{4}$ of the members of the legislature did not vote on the measure.

    (2) If 5 additional members of the legislature had voted against the measure, then the fraction of members of the legislature voting against the measure would have been $\frac{1}{3}$.

### Arithmetic Ratio and Proportion

The task in this question is to determine whether, on the basis of statements 1 and 2, it is possible to calculate the number of members of the legislature who voted against a certain measure.

(1) This statement, that $\frac{1}{4}$ of the members of the legislature did not vote on the measure, is compatible with any number of members of the legislature voting against the measure. After all, any number among the $\frac{3}{4}$ of the remaining members could have voted against the measure. Furthermore, based on statement 1, we do not know the number of members of the legislature (although we do know, based on this statement, that the number of members of the legislature is divisible by 4); NOT sufficient.

(2) This statement describes a scenario, of 5 additional members of the legislature voting against the measure, and stipulates that $\frac{1}{3}$ of the members of the legislature would have voted against the measure in the scenario. Given this condition, we know that the number of members of the legislature was divisible by 3, and that the legislature had at least 15 members (to

allow for the "5 additional members of the legislature" that could have voted against the measure, for a total of $\frac{1}{3}$ of the members voting against it). However, beyond this we know essentially nothing from statement 2. In particular, depending on the number of members of the legislature (which we have not been given), any number of members could have voted against the measure. For example, exactly one member could have voted against the measure, in which case the legislature would have had $(1 + 5) \times 3 = 18$ members. Exactly two members could have voted against the measure, in which case the legislature would have had $(2 + 5) \times 3 = 21$ members, and so on for 3 members voting against, 4 members voting against, etc.; NOT sufficient.

Considering the statements 1 and 2 together, the reasoning is similar to the reasoning for statement 2, but with the further condition that the total number of members of the legislature is divisible by 12 (so as to allow that both exactly $\frac{1}{4}$ of the members did not vote on the measure while exactly $\frac{1}{3}$ could have voted against the measure). For example, it could have been the case that the legislature had 24 members. In this case, $\frac{1}{3}$ of the members would have been 8 members, and, consistent with statements 1 and 2, 3 of the members $(8 - 5)$ could have voted against the measure. Or the legislature could have had 36 members, in which case, consistent with statements 1 and 2, $\frac{1}{3}(36) - 5 = 12 - 5 = 7$ members could have voted against the measure.

**The correct answer is E; both statements together are still not sufficient.**

38. During a certain bicycle ride, was Sherry's average speed faster than 24 kilometers per hour? (1 kilometer = 1,000 meters)

(1) Sherry's average speed during the bicycle ride was faster than 7 meters per second.

(2) Sherry's average speed during the bicycle ride was slower than 8 meters per second.

**Arithmetic Applied Problems**

This problem can be solved by converting 24 kilometers per hour into meters per second. First, 24 kilometers is equivalent to 24,000 meters and 1 hour is equivalent to 3,600 seconds. Then, traveling 24 kilometers in 1 hour is equivalent to traveling 24,000 meters in 3,600 seconds, or $\frac{24,000}{3,600} = 6\frac{2}{3}$ meters per second.

(1) This indicates that Sherry's average speed was faster than 7 meters per second, which is faster than $6\frac{2}{3}$ meters per second and, therefore, faster than 24 kilometers per hour; SUFFICIENT.

(2) This indicates that Sherry's average speed was slower than 8 meters per second. Her average speed could have been 7 meters per second (since $7 < 8$), in which case her average speed was faster than $6\frac{2}{3}$ meters per second and, therefore, faster than 24 kilometers per hour. Or her average speed could have been 5 meters per second (since $5 < 8$), in which case her average speed was not faster than $6\frac{2}{3}$ meters per second and, therefore, not faster than 24 kilometers per hour; NOT sufficient.

**The correct answer is A; statement 1 alone is sufficient.**

39. Working together, Rafael and Salvador can tabulate a certain set of data in 2 hours. In how many hours can Rafael tabulate the data working alone?

(1) Working alone, Rafael can tabulate the data in 3 hours less time than Salvador, working alone, can tabulate the data.

(2) Working alone, Rafael can tabulate the data in $\frac{1}{2}$ the time that Salvador, working alone, can tabulate the data.

**Algebra Simultaneous Equations**

We are given that Rafael and Salvador, working together, can tabulate the set of data in two hours. That is, if Rafael tabulates data at the rate of $R$ units of data per hour and Salvador tabulates the data at the rate of $S$ units per hour, then, if the set of data is made up of $D$ units, then $2R + 2S = D$. Can we determine how much time, in hours, it takes Rafael to tabulate the data if working alone?

(1) First of all, note that the choice of units used to measure the amounts of data doesn't matter. In particular, we can define one unit of data to be $D$. Thus, $2R + 2S = 1$. With this in mind, consider the condition that Rafael, when working alone, can tabulate the data in 3 hours less time than Salvador can when working alone. Given that Rafael tabulates $R$ units of data per unit time, he takes $\frac{1}{R}$ units of time to tabulate one unit of data. Similarly, Salvador takes $\frac{1}{S}$ units of time to tabulate one unit of data. This unit, as defined, is simply the entire set of data. Our given condition thus becomes $\frac{1}{R} = \frac{1}{S} - 3$, and we have the set of simultaneous equations made up of this equation and the equation $2R + 2S = 1$.

One way to determine the number of hours it would take Rafael to tabulate the data is to solve one of these equations for $S$ and then substitute this solution into the other equation. Considering the first of these equations, we multiply both sides by $RS$ and then manipulate the result as follows.

$$S = R - 3RS$$
$$S + 3RS = R$$
$$S(1 + 3R) = R$$
$$S = \frac{R}{1 + 3R}$$

Substituting into the equation $2R + 2S = 1$,

$$2R + \frac{2R}{1 + 3R} = 1$$

Multiplying both sides by $1 + 3R$ to eliminate the fraction,

$$2R(1 + 3R) + 2R = 1 + 3R$$
$$2R + 6R^2 = 1 + R$$
$$6R^2 + R - 1 = 0$$
$$(3R - 1)(2R + 1) = 0$$

This equation has two solutions, $-\frac{1}{2}$ and $\frac{1}{3}$. However, because the rate $R$ cannot be negative, we find that Rafael tabulates $\frac{1}{3}$ of a unit of data every hour. Since one unit is the entire set, it takes Rafael 3 hours to tabulate the entire set; SUFFICIENT.

(2) We are given that Rafael, working alone, can tabulate the data in $\frac{1}{2}$ the amount of time it takes Salvador, working alone, to tabulate the data. As in the discussion of statement 1, we have that Rafael tabulates $R$ units of data every hour, and takes $\frac{1}{R}$ hours to tabulate one unit of data. Similarly, it takes Salvador $\frac{1}{S}$ hours to tabulate one unit of data. One unit of data has been defined to be the size of the entire set to be tabulated, so statement 2 becomes the expression

$$\frac{1}{R} = \frac{1}{2} \times \frac{1}{S} = \frac{1}{2S}$$

We thus have $2S = R$. Substituting this value for $2S$ in the equation $2R + 2S = 1$, we have $R + 2R = 1$, and $3R = 1$. Solving for $R$ we get $\frac{1}{3}$; SUFFICIENT.

Note that, for both statements 1 and 2, it would have been possible to stop calculating once we had determined whether it was possible to find a unique value for $R$. The ability to make such judgments accurately is part of what the test has been designed to measure.

**The correct answer is D; each statement alone is sufficient.**

40. Yesterday between 9:00 a.m. and 6:00 p.m. at Airport X, all flights to Atlanta departed at equally spaced times and all flights to New York City departed at equally spaced times. A flight to Atlanta and a flight to New York City both departed from Airport X at 1:00 p.m. yesterday. Between 1:00 p.m. and 3:00 p.m. yesterday, did another pair of flights to these 2 cities depart from Airport X at the same time?

(1) Yesterday at Airport X, a flight to Atlanta and a flight to New York City both departed at 10:00 a.m.

(2) Yesterday at Airport X, flights to New York City departed every 15 minutes between 9:00 a.m. and 6:00 p.m.

**Arithmetic Applied Problems**

It is useful to note that although the departures discussed all lie between 9:00 a.m. and 6:00 p.m., there is no information concerning when the first departures took place during this time other than what is necessary for the information to be consistent. For example, since departures to both Atlanta and New York City took place at 1:00 p.m., the first departure to either of these cities could not have occurred after 1:00 p.m.

(1) Given that departures to both Atlanta and New York City took place at 10:00 a.m., it is not possible to determine whether simultaneous departures to these cities occurred between 1:00 p.m. and 3:00 p.m. For example, it is possible that departures to both Atlanta and New York City took place every 15 minutes beginning at 9:15 a.m., and thus it is possible that simultaneous departures to both these cities occurred between 1:00 p.m. and 3:00 p.m. However, it is also possible that departures to Atlanta took place every 3 hours beginning at 10:00 a.m. and departures to New York City took place every 15 minutes beginning at 9:15 a.m., and thus it is possible that no simultaneous departures to these cities occurred between 1:00 p.m. and 3:00 p.m.; NOT sufficient.

(2) Given that departures to New York City took place every 15 minutes, the same examples used in (1) can be used to show that it is not possible to determine whether simultaneous departures to these cities occurred between 1:00 p.m. and 3:00 p.m.; NOT sufficient.

Taking (1) and (2) together, it is still not possible to determine whether simultaneous departures to these cities occurred between 1:00 p.m. and 3:00 p.m. because both (1) and (2) are true for the examples above.

**The correct answer is E;
both statements together are still not sufficient.**

41. Of the total number of copies of Magazine X sold last week, 40 percent were sold at full price. What was the total number of copies of the magazine sold last week?

(1) Last week, full price for a copy of Magazine X was $1.50 and the total revenue from full-price sales was $112,500.

(2) The total number of copies of Magazine X sold last week at full price was $75,000.

**Algebra Applied Problems**

For the copies of Magazine X sold last week, let $n$ be the total number of copies sold and let $\$p$ be the full price of each copy. Then for Magazine X last week, a total of $0.4n$ copies were each sold at price $\$p$. What is the value of $n$ ?

(1) Given that $\$p = 1.50$ and $(0.4n)(\$p) = \$112{,}500$, it follows that $(0.4n)(1.5) = 112{,}500$, or $0.6n = 112{,}500$, or $n = \dfrac{112{,}500}{0.6}$; SUFFICIENT.

(2) Given that $0.4n = 75{,}000$, it follows that $n = \dfrac{75{,}000}{0.4}$; SUFFICIENT.

**The correct answer is D;
each statement alone is sufficient.**

42. What is the average (arithmetic mean) annual salary of the 6 employees of a toy company?

(1) If the 6 annual salaries were ordered from least to greatest, each annual salary would be $6,300 greater than the preceding annual salary.

(2) The range of the 6 annual salaries is $31,500.

**Arithmetic Statistics**

Can we determine the arithmetic mean of the annual salaries of the 6 employees?

(1) Given only that the 6 annual salaries can be put into a sequence from least to greatest, with a difference of $6,300 between adjacent members of the sequence, we can infer certain things about the mean of the salaries. For example, because none of the salaries would be negative, we know from statement 1 that the mean of the salaries is greater than or equal to

$$\frac{0 + \$6{,}300 + \$12{,}600 + \$18{,}900 + \$25{,}200 + \$31{,}500}{6}.$$

(It is not necessary to perform this calculation.) However, depending on what the least of the salaries is—that is, the value at which the sequence of salaries begins—the average of the salaries could, consistent with condition 1, take on any value greater than this quotient; NOT sufficient.

(2) Given the statement that the range of the salaries is $31,500, reasoning similar to the reasoning for statement 1 applies. A difference between least salary and greatest salary of $31,500 is consistent with any value for the least salary, so long as the greatest salary is $31,500 greater than the least salary. Furthermore, even if we knew what the least and the greatest salaries are, it would be impossible to determine the mean merely from the range; NOT sufficient.

As reflected in the numerator of the quotient in the discussion of statement 1, we can see that statement 1 implies statement 2. In the sequence of 6 salaries with a difference of $6,300 between adjacent members of the sequence, the difference between the least salary and the greatest salary is $5 \times \$6,300 = \$31,500$. Therefore, because statement 1 is insufficient for determining the mean of the salaries, the combination of statement 1 and statement 2 is also insufficient for determining the mean of the salaries.

**The correct answer is E; both statements together are not sufficient.**

43. In a certain order, the pretax price of each regular pencil was $0.03, the pretax price of each deluxe pencil was $0.05, and there were 50% more deluxe pencils than regular pencils. All taxes on the order are a fixed percent of the pretax prices. The sum of the total pretax price of the order and the tax on the order was $44.10. What was the amount, in dollars, of the tax on the order?

    (1) The tax on the order was 5% of the total pretax price of the order.
    (2) The order contained exactly 400 regular pencils.

**Arithmetic Percents**

Let $n$ be the number of regular pencils in the order and let $r\%$ be the tax rate on the order as a percent of the pretax

price. Then the order contains $1.5n$ deluxe pencils, the total pretax price of the order is $(\$0.03)n + (\$0.05)(1.5n) = \$0.105n$, and the sum of the total pretax price of the order and the tax on the order is $\left(1+\dfrac{r}{100}\right)(\$0.105n)$. Given that $\left(1+\dfrac{r}{100}\right)(\$0.105n) = \$44.10$, what is the value of $\left(\dfrac{r}{100}\right)(\$0.105n)$ ?

(1) Given that $r = 5$, then $\left(1+\dfrac{r}{100}\right)(\$0.105n)$ = \$44.10$ becomes $(1.05)(0.105n) = 44.10$, which is a first-degree equation that can be solved for $n$. Since the value of $r$ is known and the value of $n$ can be determined, it follows that the value of $\left(\dfrac{r}{100}\right)(\$0.105n)$ can be determined; SUFFICIENT.

(2) Given that $n = 400$, then

$\left(1+\dfrac{r}{100}\right)(\$0.105n) = \$44.10$ becomes

$\left(1+\dfrac{r}{100}\right)(0.105)(400) = 44.10$, which is a first-degree equation that can be solved for $r$. Since the value of $r$ can be determined and the value of $n$ is known, it follows that the value of $\left(\dfrac{r}{100}\right)(\$0.105n)$ can be determined; SUFFICIENT.

**The correct answer is D; each statement alone is sufficient.**

44. A total of 20 amounts are entered on a spreadsheet that has 5 rows and 4 columns; each of the 20 positions in the spreadsheet contains one amount. The average (arithmetic mean) of the amounts in row $i$ is $R_i$ ($1 \le i \le 5$). The average of the amounts in column $j$ is $C_j$ ($1 \le j \le 4$). What is the average of all 20 amounts on the spreadsheet?

    (1) $R_1 + R_2 + R_3 + R_4 + R_5 = 550$
    (2) $C_1 + C_2 + C_3 + C_4 = 440$

**Arithmetic Statistics**

It is given that $R_i$ represents the average of the amounts in row $i$. Since there are four amounts in each row, $4R_i$ represents the total of the amounts in row $i$. Likewise, it is given that $C_j$ represents the average of the amounts in column $j$. Since there are five amounts in each column, $5C_j$ represents the total of the amounts in column $j$.

(1) It is given that $R_1 + R_2 + R_3 + R_4 + R_5 = 550$, and so $4(R_1 + R_2 + R_3 + R_4 + R_5) = 4R_1 + 4R_2 + 4R_3 + 4R_4 + 4R_5 = 4(550) = 2,200$. Therefore, 2,200 is the sum of all 20 amounts (4 amounts in each of 5 rows), and the average of all 20 amounts is $\frac{2,200}{20} = 110$; SUFFICIENT.

(2) It is given that $C_1 + C_2 + C_3 + C_4 = 440$, and so $5(C_1 + C_2 + C_3 + C_4) = 5C_1 + 5C_2 + 5C_3 + 5C_4 = 5(440) = 2,200$. Therefore, 2,200 is the sum of all 20 amounts (5 amounts in each of 4 columns), and the average of all 20 amounts is $\frac{2,200}{20} = 110$; SUFFICIENT.

**The correct answer is D;
each statement alone is sufficient.**

45. Was the range of the amounts of money that Company Y budgeted for its projects last year equal to the range of the amounts of money that it budgeted for its projects this year?

(1) Both last year and this year, Company Y budgeted money for 12 projects and the least amount of money that it budgeted for a project was $400.

(2) Both last year and this year, the average (arithmetic mean) amount of money that Company Y budgeted per project was $2,000.

**Arithmetic Statistics**

Let $G_1$ and $L_1$ represent the greatest and least amounts, respectively, of money that Company Y budgeted for its projects last year, and let $G_2$ and $L_2$ represent the greatest and least amounts, respectively, of money that Company Y budgeted for its projects this year. Determine if the range of the amounts of money Company Y budgeted for its projects last year is equal to the range of amounts budgeted for its projects this year; that is, determine if $G_1 - L_1 = G_2 - L_2$.

(1) This indicates that $L_1 = L_2 = \$400$, but does not give any information about $G_1$ or $G_2$; NOT sufficient.

(2) This indicates that the average amount Company Y budgeted for its projects both last year and this year was $2,000 per project, but does not give any information about the least and greatest amounts that it budgeted for its projects either year; NOT sufficient.

Taking (1) and (2) together, it is known that $L_1 = L_2 = \$400$ and that the average amount Company Y budgeted for its projects both last year and this year was $2,000 per project, but there is no information about $G_1$ or $G_2$. For example, if, for each year, Company Y budgeted $400 for each of 2 projects and $2,320 for each of the 10 others, then (1) and (2) are true and the range for each year was $2,320 - \$400 = \$1,920$. However, if, last year, Company Y budgeted $400 for each of 2 projects and $2,320 for each of the 10 others, and, this year, budgeted $400 for each of 11 projects and $19,600 for 1 project, then (1) and (2) are true, but the range for last year was $1,920 and the range for this year was $19,600 - \$400 = \$19,200$.

**The correct answer is E;
both statements together are still not sufficient.**

46. What is the probability that Lee will make exactly 5 errors on a certain typing test?

(1) The probability that Lee will make 5 or more errors on the test is 0.27.

(2) The probability that Lee will make 5 or fewer errors on the test is 0.85.

**Arithmetic Probability**

(1) Given that 0.27 is the probability that Lee will make 5 or more errors on the test, it is clearly not possible to determine the probability that Lee will make exactly 5 errors on the test; NOT sufficient.

(2) Given that 0.85 is the probability that Lee will make 5 or fewer errors on the test, it is clearly not possible to determine the probability that Lee will make exactly 5 errors on the test; NOT sufficient.

Taking (1) and (2) together, let $E$ be the event that Lee will make 5 or more errors on the test and let $F$ be the event that Lee will make 5 or fewer errors on the test. Then $P(E \text{ or } F) = 1$, since it will always be the case that, when taking the test, Lee will make at least 5 errors or at most 5 errors. Also, (1) and (2) can be expressed as $P(E) = 0.27$ and $P(F) = 0.85$, and the question asks for the value of $P(E \text{ and } F)$. Using the identity $P(E \text{ or } F) = P(E) + P(F) - P(E \text{ and } F)$, it follows that $1 = 0.27 + 0.85 - P(E \text{ and } F)$, or $P(E \text{ and } F) = 0.27 + 0.85 - 1 = 0.12$. Therefore, the probability that Lee will make exactly 5 errors on the test is 0.12.

**The correct answer is C;
both statements together are sufficient.**

47. A small factory that produces only upholstered chairs and sofas uses 1 cushion for each chair and 4 cushions for each sofa. If the factory used a total of 300 cushions on the furniture it produced last week, how many sofas did it produce last week?

    (1) Last week the factory produced more chairs than sofas.

    (2) Last week the factory produced a total of 150 chairs and sofas.

**Algebra Simultaneous Equations**

Let $c$ and $s$ be the numbers, respectively, of chairs and sofas produced last week. From the information given about the cushions used last week, we have $c + 4s = 300$. Can we determine the value of $s$ ?

    (1) Given that $c > s$, it is not possible to determine the value of $s$. For example, it is possible that $c = 200$ and $s = 25$ (for these values, $c > s$ and $c + 4s = 200 + 4(25) = 300$) and it is possible that $c = 100$ and $s = 50$ (for these values, $c > s$ and $c + 4s = 100 + 4(50) = 300$); NOT sufficient.

    (2) Given that $c + s = 150$, by subtracting this equation from $c + 4s = 300$ we get $(c + 4s) - (c + s) = 300 - 150$, or $3s = 150$. Therefore, $s = 50$; SUFFICIENT.

**The correct answer is B;
statement 2 alone is sufficient.**

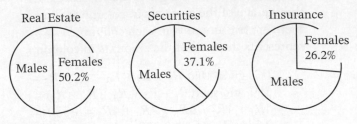

DISTRIBUTION OF SALESPERSONS
BY GENDER IN THREE SECTORS, YEAR $X$

48. In year $X$ were there more female salespersons in the securities sector than in the insurance sector?

    (1) There were more male salespersons in the insurance sector than in the securities sector.

    (2) The total number of salespersons was greater in the securities sector than in the insurance sector.

**Arithmetic Percents**

From the graphs, 37.1% of the salespersons in securities are females and $(100 - 37.1)\% = 62.9\%$ are males; 26.2% of the salespersons in insurance are females and $(100 - 26.2)\% = 73.8\%$ are males. Let $S$ and $I$ represent the number of salespersons in securities and insurance, respectively. Let $F_S$, $M_S$, $F_I$, and $M_I$, represent the numbers of female and male salespersons, respectively, in securities and insurance, respectively. Determine if the inequality $F_S > F_I$ is true.

    (1) Given that $M_I > M_S$, it is not possible to determine if $F_S > F_I$ is true. For example, if $S = 10,000$ and $I = 9,000$, then $M_S = 0.629(10,000) = 6,290$, $M_I = 0.738(9,000) = 6,642$, $F_S = 0.371(10,000) = 3,710$, and $F_I = 0.262(9,000) = 2,358$. These numbers are summarized in the table below, from which it is easy to see that $M_I > M_S$ and $F_S > F_I$.

| Sector | Number of employees | Males | Females |
|---|---|---|---|
| Securities | 10,000 | 6,290 | 3,710 |
| Insurance | 9,000 | 6,642 | 2,358 |

However, if $S = 10,000$ and $I = 20,000$, then $M_S = 0.629(10,000) = 6,290$, $M_I = 0.738(20,000) = 14,760$,

$F_S = 0.371(10,000) = 3,710$ and $F_I = 0.262(20,000) = 5,240$. These numbers are summarized in the table below, from which it is easy to see that $M_I > M_S$ and $F_S < F_I$; NOT sufficient.

| Sector | Number of employees | Males | Females |
|--------|---------------------|-------|---------|
| Securities | 10,000 | 6,290 | 3,710 |
| Insurance | 20,000 | 14,760 | 5,240 |

(1) Given that $S > I$, it follows that $0.371S > 0.371I$ and $0.371I > 0.262I$, so $0.371S > 0.262I$ and $F_S > F_I$; SUFFICIENT.

**The correct answer is B; statement 2 alone is sufficient.**

49. If a club made a gross profit of $0.25 for each candy bar it sold, how many candy bars did the club sell?

(1) The total revenue from the sale of the candy bars was $300.

(2) If the club had sold 80 more candy bars, its gross profits would have increased by 20 percent.

**Algebra First-Degree Equations**

Let $n$ be the number of candy bars sold. The gross profit from selling the $n$ candy bars was $0.25n$. What is the value of $n$, or equivalently, what is the value of $0.25n$?

(1) Given that the total revenue was $300, it is not possible to determine how many candy bars the club sold because nothing is known about the total cost, which is the value of $300 - 0.25n$; NOT sufficient.

(2) Given that the gross profit from selling $(n + 80)$ candy bars is equal to $(1.2)(0.25n)$, it follows that $(0.25)(n + 80) = (1.2)(0.25n)$. Therefore, $0.25n + 20 = (1.2)(0.25n)$, or $20 = (0.2)(0.25n)$, and hence $0.25n = 100$; SUFFICIENT.

**The correct answer is B; statement 2 alone is sufficient.**

50. In one year 2,100 malpractice claims were filed with insurance company X and of these $\frac{1}{4}$ resulted in a financial settlement. Of those resulting in a financial settlement of less than $400,000, what was the average payment per claim?

(1) Company X paid a total of 24.5 million dollars to the claimants.

(2) Only 5 claims resulted in payments of $400,000 or more.

**Arithmetic Statistics**

A total of $\frac{1}{4}(2,100) = 525$ claims were paid. What was the average payment per claim of those claims having a payment less than $400,000 ?

(1) Given that the total payment for the 525 paid claims was $24.5 million, it is not possible to determine the average payment per claim. This is because almost nothing is known about the total payment for those claims less than $400,000 or the number of those claims less than $400,000 (we only know they cannot exceed $24.5 million and 525 paid claims), and thus, more than one value is possible for the average payment per claim for those claims less than $400,000; NOT sufficient.

(2) Given that a total of 5 paid claims had payments of $400,000 or greater, it is not possible to determine the average payment per claim. This is because nothing is known about the total payment for those claims less than $400,000, and thus, more than one value is possible for this total payment divided by 520 (i.e., the average payment per claim for those claims less than $400,000); NOT sufficient.

Taking (1) and (2) together, it is still not possible to determine the average payment per claim. For example, if each of the 5 paid claims of over $400,000 was equal to $500,000, then the average payment per claim for those claims less than $400,000 would be $\frac{\$24.5 \text{ million} - \$2.5 \text{ million}}{520} = \frac{\$22 \text{ million}}{520}$. However, if each of the 5 paid claims of over $400,000 was equal to $4 million, then the average payment per claim for those claims less than $400,000 would be

$$\frac{\$24.5\ \text{million} - \$20\ \text{million}}{520} = \frac{\$4.5\ \text{million}}{520},$$

which is different from the first example.

**The correct answer is E;**
**both statements together are still not sufficient.**

51.  If there are 13 boys in club X, what is the average age of these boys?

(1)  The oldest boy is 13 years old and the youngest boy is 9 years old.

(2)  Eleven of the boys are either 10 years old or 11 years old.

**Arithmetic** Statistics

What is the average age of the 13 boys, or equivalently, what is the sum of the ages of the 13 boys?

(1)  Given that the oldest boy is 13 and the youngest boy is 9, it is not possible to determine the sum of their ages. For example, if their ages were such that one is 9, eleven are 10, and one is 13, then the sum of their ages would be less than if their ages were such that one is 9, eleven are 11, and one is 13; NOT sufficient.

(2)  Given that eleven of the boys are either 10 or 11, it is not possible to determine the sum of their ages, because the same examples used above are such that eleven of the boys are either 10 or 11; NOT sufficient.

Taking (1) and (2) together, it is not possible to determine the sum of their ages because the examples above satisfy both (1) and (2).

**The correct answer is E;**
**both statements together are still not sufficient.**

52.  If all the employees of a company fall into one and only one of 3 groups, X, Y, or Z, with 250, 100, and 20 members in each group, respectively, what is the average (arithmetic mean) weekly salary of all the employees of this company, if all employees are paid every week of the year?

(1)  The average (arithmetic mean) annual salary of the employees in Group X is $10,000, in Group Y $15,000 and in Group Z $20,000.

(2)  The total annual payroll is $4,400,000.

**Arithmetic** Statistics

The average of the weekly salaries is the average of the annual salaries divided by 52, and thus the average of the weekly salaries can be determined if and only if the average of the annual salaries can be determined. What is the average of the annual salaries, or equivalently, what is the sum of the annual salaries?

(1)  Given that the average of the annual salaries of employees in Groups X, Y, and Z is $10,000, $15,000, and $20,000, respectively, it follows that the sum of the annual salaries of employees in Groups X, Y, and Z is 250($10,000), 100($15,000), and 20($20,000), respectively. Therefore, the sum of the annual salaries is the sum of these three amounts; SUFFICIENT.

(2)  We are given that the sum of the annual salaries is $4,400,000; SUFFICIENT.

**The correct answer is D;**
**each statement alone is sufficient.**

DISTRIBUTION OF SALES INCOME
FOR STORE *S* LAST WEEK

100% = $100,000

53.  According to the graph above, the sale of fruits and vegetables in Store *S* last week accounted for what percent of the total sales income for the week?

(1)  Last week the total income from the sale of fruits and vegetables in Store S was $16,000.

(2)  x = 2y

**Algebra** Percents

According to the graph, sales of fruits and vegetables accounted for x% of the total sales, baked goods accounted for $y\%$, and all other categories combined accounted for 76%. It follows that $x + y = 100 - 76 = 24$. Determine the value of $x$.

(1)  Given that sales of fruits and vegetables accounted for $x\%$ of the total sales of \$100,000 and this amounted to \$16,000, it follows that $\frac{x}{100}(100,000) = 16,000$. Thus, $x = 16$; SUFFICIENT.

(2)  Given that $x = 2y$, it follows that $x + y = 3y = 24$, $y = 8$, and $x = 16$; SUFFICIENT.

**The correct answer is D; each statement alone is sufficient.**

54.  Larry saves x dollars per month. Will Larry's total savings one year from now exceed his present savings by at least $500 ? (Assume that there is no interest.)

(1)  In 6 months Larry's total savings will be $900.

(2)  In 3 months Larry's total savings will exceed his present savings by $150.

**Algebra Applied Problems**

Let \$$p$ be Larry's present savings. Larry saves \$$x$ per month. One year from now (i.e., 12 months from now), Larry will have saved an additional \$$12x$. Determine if $(p + 12x) - p > 500$ or, equivalently, determine if $12x > 500$.

(1)  Given that in 6 months Larry will have saved a total of \$900, it follows that $p + 6x = 900$, but since the value of $p$ is unknown, it cannot be determined if $12x > 500$; NOT sufficient.

(2)  Given that $(p + 3x) - p = \$150$, it follows that $x = 50$, $12x = 600$, and $12x > 500$; SUFFICIENT.

**The correct answer is B; statement 2 alone is sufficient.**

55.  If Randy has twice as many coins as Alice, and if Maria has 7 times as many coins as Alice, what is the combined number of coins that all three of them have?

(1)  Alice has 4 fewer coins than Randy.

(2)  Maria has 20 more coins than Randy.

**Algebra Simultaneous Equations**

Determine the total number of coins that Randy, Alice, and Maria have, given that Randy has twice as many coins as Alice and Maria has 7 times as many coins as Alice. In other words, determine the value of $R + A + M$, where $R$, $A$, and $M$ represent the number of coins, respectively, that Randy, Alice, and Maria have, given that $R = 2A$ and $M = 7A$.

(1)  Given that Alice has 4 fewer coins than Randy, it follows that $A = R - 4$. Since $R = 2A$, it follows that $A = 2A - 4$, from which the value of $A$ can be determined. From the value of $A$, values for $R$ and $M$ can be determined and $R + A + M$ can also be determined; SUFFICIENT.

(2)  Given that Maria has 20 more coins than Randy, it follows that $M = R + 20$. Since $M = 7A$ and $R = 2A$, it follows that $7A = 2A + 20$, from which the value of $A$ can be determined. From the value of $A$, values for $R$ and $M$ can be determined and $R + A + M$ can also be determined; SUFFICIENT.

**The correct answer is D; each statement alone is sufficient.**

56.  A line of people waiting to enter a theater consists of seven separate and successive groups. The first person in each group purchases one ticket for each person in the group and for no one else. If n is the total number of tickets sold for the first six groups, is n an even number?

(1)  There are no more than 4 people in each group.

(2)  The 19th person in line purchases the tickets for the seventh group.

**Arithmetic Applied Problems**

Determine whether the total number of people in the first six groups is an even number.

(1)  Given that each group contains at most 4 people, it is not possible to determine whether the total number of people in the first six groups is an even number. For example, if the numbers of people in the first six groups were 2, 2, 2, 2, 2, and 2, then the total number of people in the first

six groups would be 12, which is an even number. However, if the numbers of people in the first six groups were 2, 2, 2, 2, 2, and 3, then the total number of people in the first six groups would be 13, which is not an even number; NOT sufficient.

(2) Given that the 19th person in line purchased the tickets for the seventh group, it follows that the total number of people in the first six groups was 18, which is an even number; SUFFICIENT.

**The correct answer is B;**
**statement 2 alone is sufficient.**

57. If John has exactly 10 coins each of which was minted in 1910 or 1920 or 1930, how many of his coins were minted in 1920 ?

(1) Exactly 6 of his coins were minted in 1910 or 1920.

(2) Exactly 7 of his coins were minted in 1920 or 1930.

**Algebra** Simultaneous Equations

Let $x$, $y$, and $z$ be the numbers of coins John has that were minted in, respectively, 1910, 1920, and 1930. Then $x$, $y$, and $z$ are nonnegative integers and $x + y + z = 10$. What is the value of $y$ ?

(1) Given that $x + y = 6$, it is possible that $y = 2$ (for example, $x = 4$, $y = 2$, and $z = 4$) and it is possible that $y = 4$ (for example, $x = 2$, $y = 4$, and $z = 4$); NOT sufficient.

(2) Given that $y + z = 7$, it is possible that $y = 3$ (for example, $x = 3$, $y = 3$, and $z = 4$) and it is possible that $y = 4$ (for example, $x = 3$, $y = 4$, and $z = 3$); NOT sufficient.

Taking (1) and (2) together, from $x + y + z = 10$ and (1) it follows that $6 + z = 10$, or $z = 4$. Substituting $z = 4$ into $y + z = 7$ gives $y + 4 = 7$, or $y = 3$.

**The correct answer is C;**
**both statements together are sufficient.**

58. The total profit of corporation K was $3,400,000 in year X. What was the total profit in year Y ?

(1) Income in year Y was 30 percent more than in year X.

(2) Costs in year Y were 40 percent more than in year X.

**Algebra** Applied Problems

Let $\$C_X$ be costs in year X, $\$I_X$ be income in year X, $\$C_Y$ be costs in year Y, and $\$I_Y$ be income in year Y. Given that $I_X - C_X = 3,400,000$, determine the value of $I_Y - C_Y$.

(1) Given that $I_Y = 1.3I_X$, some information about income in year Y is known, but since nothing is known about costs in year Y, the profit in year Y cannot be determined; NOT sufficient.

(2) Given that $C_Y = 1.4C_X$, some information about costs in year Y is known, but since nothing is known about income in year Y, the profit in year Y cannot be determined; NOT sufficient.

Taking (1) and (2) together, $I_Y - C_Y = 1.3I_X - 1.4C_X = 1.3(I_X - C_X) - 0.1C_X = 1.3(3,400,000) - 0.1C_X$, which can have more than one possible value. The table below gives two specific examples that illustrate this.

| $C_X$ | 1,000,000 | 2,000,000 |
|---|---|---|
| $I_X$ | 4,400,000 | 5,400,000 |
| $I_X - C_X$ | 3,400,000 | 3,400,000 |
| $C_Y = 1.4C_X$ | 1,400,000 | 2,800,000 |
| $I_Y = 1.3I_X$ | 5,720,000 | 7,020,000 |
| $I_Y - C_Y$ | 4,320,000 | 4,220,000 |

**The correct answer is E;**
**both statements together are still not sufficient.**

59. Zelma scored 90, 88, and 92 on 3 of the 6 mathematics tests that she took. What was her average (arithmetic mean) score on the 6 tests?

(1) Her average (arithmetic mean) score on 5 of the tests was 90.

(2) Her score on one of the tests was 91.

**Arithmetic** Statistics

Determine the average (arithmetic mean) of Zelma's 6 test scores given that 3 of the scores are 90, 88, and 92.

(1) Given that the average score on 5 of the 6 tests was 90, it is not possible to determine the average of all 6 test scores. For example, the 6 test scores could be 89, 91, 90, 88, 92, and 100 for an average score of $91\frac{2}{3}$ or the 6 test scores could be 89, 91, 90, 88, 92, and 50 for an average score of $83\frac{1}{3}$; NOT sufficient.

(2) Given that one of the scores was 91, it is not possible to determine the average of all 6 test scores. For example, the 6 test scores could be 89, 91, 90, 88, 92, and 100 for an average score of $91\frac{2}{3}$ or the 6 test scores could be 89, 91, 90, 88, 92, and 50 for an average score of $88\frac{1}{3}$; NOT sufficient.

Taking (1) and (2) together and noting that the examples that were used to show that (2) is not sufficient were the same examples that were used to show that (1) is not sufficient, the average of Zelma's 6 test scores cannot be determined.

**The correct answer is E; both statements together are still not sufficient.**

## Questions 60 to 83 - Difficulty: **Hard**

60. What percent of the students at University X are enrolled in a science course but are not enrolled in a biology course?

    (1) 28 percent of the students at University X are enrolled in a biology course.

    (2) 70 percent of the students at University X who are enrolled in a science course are enrolled in a biology course.

**Algebra Percents**

Under the assumption that a biology course is a type of science course, determine the percent of University X students who are enrolled in a science course, but not in a biology course.

(1) Given that 28% of the students at University X are enrolled in a biology course, if 100% of the students are enrolled in a science course, then $(100 − 28)\% = 72\%$ are enrolled in a science course, but not in

a biology course. On the other hand if 50% of the students at University X are enrolled in a science course, then $(50 − 28)\% = 22\%$ are enrolled in a science course, but not in a biology course; NOT sufficient.

(2) Given that 70% of the students at University X who are enrolled in a science course are enrolled in a biology course, if 100% of the students at University X are enrolled in a science course, then $(100 − 70)\% = 30\%$ are enrolled in a science course, but not in a biology course. On the other hand if 50% of the students at University X are enrolled in a science course, then 70% of 50% = 35% are enrolled in a biology course, $(50 − 35)\% = 15\%$ are enrolled in a science course, but not in a biology course; NOT sufficient.

Taking (1) and (2) together, $0.28 = 0.7x$ where $x$ is the percent of the students at University X who are enrolled in a science course. It follows that $x = 0.4$ or 40%. Thus, $(40 − 28)\% − 12\%$ of the students at University X are enrolled in a science course, but not in a biology course.

**The correct answer is C; both statements together are sufficient.**

61. Each Type A machine fills 400 cans per minute, each Type B machine fills 600 cans per minute, and each Type C machine installs 2,400 lids per minute. A lid is installed on each can that is filled and on no can that is not filled. For a particular minute, what is the total number of machines working?

    (1) A total of 4,800 cans are filled that minute.

    (2) For that minute, there are 2 Type B machines working for every Type C machine working.

**Algebra Simultaneous Equations**

(1) Given that 4,800 cans were filled that minute, it is possible that 12 Type A machines, no Type B machines, and 2 Type C machines were working, for a total of 14 machines, since $(12)(400) + (0)(600) = 4,800$ and $(2)(2,400) = 4,800$. However, it is also possible that no Type A machines, 8 Type B machines, and 2 Type C machines were

working, for a total of 10 machines, since $(0)(400) + (8)(600) = 4,800$ and $(2)(2,400) = 4,800$; NOT sufficient.

(2) Given that there are 2 Type B machines working for every Type C machine working, it is possible that there are 6 machines working—3 Type A machines, 2 Type B machines, and 1 Type C machine. This gives $3(400) + 2(600) = 2,400$ cans and $1(2,400) = 2,400$ lids. It is also possible that there are 12 machines working—6 Type A machines, 4 Type B machines, and 2 Type C machines. This gives $6(400) + 4(600) = 4,800$ cans and $2(2,400) = 4,800$ lids; NOT sufficient.

Taking (1) and (2) together, since there were 4,800 cans filled that minute, there were 4,800 lids installed that minute. It follows that 2 Type C machines were working that minute, since $(2)(2,400) = 4,800$. Since there were twice this number of Type B machines working that minute, it follows that 4 Type B machines were working that minute. These 4 Type B machines filled $(4)(600) = 2,400$ cans that minute, leaving $4,800 - 2,400 = 2,400$ cans to be filled by Type A machines. Therefore, the number of Type A machines working that minute was $\frac{2,400}{400} = 6$, and it follows that the total number of machines working that minute was $2 + 4 + 6 = 12$.

**The correct answer is C; both statements together are sufficient.**

62. In a two-month survey of shoppers, each shopper bought one of two brands of detergent, X or Y, in the first month and again bought one of these brands in the second month. In the survey, 90 percent of the shoppers who bought Brand X in the first month bought Brand X again in the second month, while 60 percent of the shoppers who bought Brand Y in the first month bought Brand Y again in the second month. What percent of the shoppers bought Brand Y in the second month?

   (1) In the first month, 50 percent of the shoppers bought Brand X.

   (2) The total number of shoppers surveyed was 5,000.

**Arithmetic** Percents

This problem can be solved by using the following contingency table where $A$ and $B$ represent,

respectively, the number of shoppers who bought Brand X and the number of shoppers who bought Brand Y in the first month; $C$ and $D$ represent, respectively, the number of shoppers who bought Brand X and the number of shoppers who bought Brand Y in the second month; and $T$ represents the total number of shoppers in the survey. Also in the table, $0.9A$ represents the 90% of the shoppers who bought Brand X in the first month and also bought it in the second month, and $0.1A$ represents the $(100 - 90)\% = 10\%$ of the shoppers who bought Brand X in the first month and Brand Y in the second month. Similarly, $0.6B$ represents the 60% of the shoppers who bought Brand Y in the first month and also bought it in the second month, and $0.4B$ represents the $(100 - 60)\% = 40\%$ of the shoppers who bought Brand Y in the first month and Brand X in the second month.

| | | Second Month | | |
|---|---|---|---|---|
| | | X | Y | Total |
| First Month | X | $0.9A$ | $0.1A$ | $A$ |
| | Y | $0.4B$ | $0.6B$ | $B$ |
| | Total | $C$ | $D$ | $T$ |

Determine the value of $\frac{D}{T}$ as a percentage.

(1) This indicates that 50% of the shoppers bought Brand X in the first month, so $A = 0.5T$. It follows that the other 50% of the shoppers bought Brand Y in the first month, so $B = 0.5T$. Then, $D = 0.1A + 0.6B = 0.1(0.5T) + 0.6(0.5T) = 0.05T + 0.30T = 0.35T$. It follows that $\frac{D}{T} = \frac{0.35T}{T} = 0.35$, which is 35%; SUFFICIENT.

(2) This indicates that $T = 5,000$, as shown in the following table:

| | | Second Month | | |
|---|---|---|---|---|
| | | X | Y | Total |
| First Month | X | $0.9A$ | $0.1A$ | $A$ |
| | Y | $0.4B$ | $0.6B$ | $B$ |
| | Total | $C$ | $D$ | 5,000 |

But not enough information is given to be able to determine $D$ or $D$ as a percentage of 5,000; NOT sufficient.

**The correct answer is A;**
**statement 1 alone is sufficient.**

63. If the total price of $n$ equally priced shares of a certain stock was $12,000, what was the price per share of the stock?

    (1) If the price per share of the stock had been $1 more, the total price of the $n$ shares would have been $300 more.

    (2) If the price per share of the stock had been $2 less, the total price of the $n$ shares would have been 5 percent less.

**Arithmetic** Arithmetic Operations; Percents

Since the price per share of the stock can be expressed as $\dfrac{\$12,000}{n}$, determining the value of $n$ is sufficient to answer this question.

    (1) A per-share increase of $1 and a total increase of $300 for $n$ shares of stock mean together that $n(\$1) = \$300$. It follows that $n = 300$; SUFFICIENT.

    (2) If the price of each of the $n$ shares had been reduced by $2, the total reduction in price would have been 5 percent less or $0.05(\$12,000)$. The equation $2n = 0.05(\$12,000)$ expresses this relationship. The value of $n$ can be determined to be 300 from this equation; SUFFICIENT.

**The correct answer is D;**
**each statement alone is sufficient.**

64. In Year X, 8.7 percent of the men in the labor force were unemployed in June compared with 8.4 percent in May. If the number of men in the labor force was the same for both months, how many men were unemployed in June of that year?

    (1) In May of Year X, the number of unemployed men in the labor force was 3.36 million.

    (2) In Year X, 120,000 more men in the labor force were unemployed in June than in May.

**Arithmetic** Percents

Since 8.7 percent of the men in the labor force were unemployed in June, the number of unemployed men could be calculated if the total number of men in the labor force was known. Let $t$ represent the total number of men in the labor force.

    (1) This implies that for May $(8.4\%)t = 3,360,000$, from which the value of $t$ can be determined; SUFFICIENT.

    (2) This implies that $(8.7\% - 8.4\%)t = 120,000$ or $(0.3\%)t = 120,000$. This equation can be solved for $t$; SUFFICIENT.

**The correct answer is D;**
**each statement alone is sufficient.**

65. On Monday morning a certain machine ran continuously at a uniform rate to fill a production order. At what time did it completely fill the order that morning?

    (1) The machine began filling the order at 9:30 a.m.

    (2) The machine had filled $\dfrac{1}{2}$ of the order by 10:30 a.m. and $\dfrac{5}{6}$ of the order by 11:10 a.m.

**Arithmetic** Arithmetic Operations

    (1) This merely states what time the machine began filling the order; NOT sufficient.

    (2) In the 40 minutes between 10:30 a.m. and 11:10 a.m., $\dfrac{5}{6} - \dfrac{1}{2} = \dfrac{1}{3}$ of the order was filled. Therefore, the entire order was completely filled in $3 \times 40 = 120$ minutes, or 2 hours. Since half the order took 1 hour and was filled by 10:30 a.m., the second half of the order, and thus the entire order, was filled by 11:30 a.m.; SUFFICIENT.

**The correct answer is B;**
**statement 2 alone is sufficient.**

66. After winning 50 percent of the first 20 games it played, Team A won all of the remaining games it played. What was the total number of games that Team A won?

    (1) Team A played 25 games altogether.

    (2) Team A won 60 percent of all the games it played.

**Arithmetic** Percents

Let $r$ be the number of the remaining games played, all of which the team won. Since the team won $(50\%)(20) = 10$ of the first 20 games and the $r$ remaining games, the total number of games the team won is $10 + r$. Also, the total number of games the team played is $20 + r$. Determine the value of $r$.

(1) Given that the total number of games played is 25, it follows that $20 + r = 25$, or $r = 5$; SUFFICIENT.

(2) It is given that the total number of games won is $(60\%)(20 + r)$, which can be expanded as $12 + 0.6r$. Since it is also known that the number of games won is $10 + r$, it follows that $12 + 0.6r = 10 + r$. Solving this equation gives $12 - 10 = r - 0.6r$, or $2 = 0.4r$, or $r = 5$; SUFFICIENT.

**The correct answer is D;**
**each statement alone is sufficient.**

67. Michael arranged all his books in a bookcase with 10 books on each shelf and no books left over. After Michael acquired 10 additional books, he arranged all his books in a new bookcase with 12 books on each shelf and no books left over. How many books did Michael have before he acquired the 10 additional books?

(1) Before Michael acquired the 10 additional books, he had fewer than 96 books.

(2) Before Michael acquired the 10 additional books, he had more than 24 books.

## Arithmetic Properties of Numbers

If $x$ is the number of books Michael had before he acquired the 10 additional books, then $x$ is a multiple of 10. After Michael acquired the 10 additional books, he had $x + 10$ books and $x + 10$ is a multiple of 12.

(1) If $x < 96$, where $x$ is a multiple of 10, then $x = 10, 20, 30, 40, 50, 60, 70, 80,$ or $90$ and $x + 10 = 20, 30, 40, 50, 60, 70, 80, 90,$ or $100$. Since $x + 10$ is a multiple of 12, then $x + 10 = 60$ and $x = 50$; SUFFICIENT.

(2) If $x > 24$, where $x$ is a multiple of 10, then $x$ must be one of the numbers 30, 40, 50, 60, 70, 80, 90, 100, 110, …, and $x + 10$ must be one of the numbers 40, 50, 60, 70, 80, 90, 100, 110, 120, …. Since there is more than one multiple of 12 among these numbers (for example, 60 and 120), the value of

$x + 10$, and therefore the value of $x$, cannot be determined; NOT sufficient.

**The correct answer is A;**
**statement 1 alone is sufficient.**

68. Last year in a group of 30 businesses, 21 reported a net profit and 15 had investments in foreign markets. How many of the businesses did not report a net profit nor invest in foreign markets last year?

(1) Last year 12 of the 30 businesses reported a net profit and had investments in foreign markets.

(2) Last year 24 of the 30 businesses reported a net profit or invested in foreign markets, or both.

## Arithmetic Concepts of Sets

Consider the Venn diagram below in which $x$ represents the number of businesses that reported a net profit and had investments in foreign markets. Since 21 businesses reported a net profit, $21 - x$ businesses reported a net profit only. Since 15 businesses had investments in foreign markets, $15 - x$ businesses had investments in foreign markets only. Finally, since there is a total of 30 businesses, the number of businesses that did not report a net profit and did not invest in foreign markets is $30 - (21 - x + x + 15 - x) = x - 6$.

Determine the value of $x - 6$, or equivalently, the value of $x$.

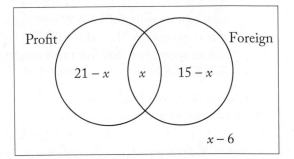

(1) It is given that $12 = x$; SUFFICIENT.

(2) It is given that $24 = (21 - x) + x + (15 - x)$. Therefore, $24 = 36 - x$, or $x = 12$.

Alternatively, the information given is exactly the number of businesses that are not among those to be counted in answering the question posed in the problem, and therefore the number of businesses that are to be counted is $30 - 24 = 6$; SUFFICIENT.

**The correct answer is D;
each statement alone is sufficient.**

69. For each landscaping job that takes more than
4 hours, a certain contractor charges a total of
$r$ dollars for the first 4 hours plus $0.2r$ dollars for each
additional hour or fraction of an hour, where $r > 100$.
Did a particular landscaping job take more than
10 hours?

    (1) The contractor charged a total of $288 for the
    job.

    (2) The contractor charged a total of $2.4r$ dollars for
    the job.

**Algebra Applied Problems**

If $y$ represents the total number of hours the
particular landscaping job took, determine if
$y > 10$.

(1) This indicates that the total charge for
the job was $288, which means that
$r + 0.2r(y - 4) = 288$. From this it cannot be
determined if $y > 10$. For example, if $r = 120$
and $y = 11$, then $120 + 0.2(120)(7) = 288$,
and the job took more than 10 hours.
However, if $r = 160$ and $y = 8$, then
$160 + 0.2(160)(4) = 288$, and the job took
less than 10 hours; NOT sufficient.

(2) This indicates that $r + 0.2r(y - 4) = 2.4r$,
from which it follows that

$r + 0.2ry - 0.8r = 2.4r$    use distributive
property

$0.2ry = 2.2r$    subtract $(r - 0.8r)$
from both sides

$y = 11$    divide both sides
by $0.2r$

Therefore, the job took more than 10 hours;
SUFFICIENT.

**The correct answer is B;
statement 2 alone is sufficient.**

70. If 75 percent of the guests at a certain banquet
ordered dessert, what percent of the guests ordered
coffee?

    (1) 60 percent of the guests who ordered dessert
    also ordered coffee.

    (2) 90 percent of the guests who ordered coffee
    also ordered dessert.

**Arithmetic Concepts of Sets; Percents**

Consider the Venn diagram below that displays
the various percentages of 4 groups of the guests.
Thus, $x$ percent of the guests ordered both dessert
and coffee and $y$ percent of the guests ordered
coffee only. Since 75 percent of the guests
ordered dessert, $(75 - x)\%$ of the guests ordered
dessert only. Also, because the 4 percentages
represented in the Venn diagram have a total
sum of 100 percent, the percentage of guests
who did not order either dessert or coffee is
$100 - [(75 - x) + x + y] = 25 - y$. Determine
the percentage of guests who ordered coffee, or
equivalently, the value of $x + y$.

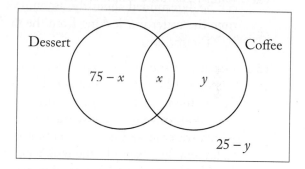

(1) Given that $x$ is equal to 60 percent of 75, or
45, the value of $x + y$ cannot be determined;
NOT sufficient.

(2) Given that 90 percent of $x + y$ is equal to $x$,
it follows that $0.9(x + y) = x$, or $9(x + y) = 10x$.
Therefore, $9x + 9y = 10x$, or $9y = x$. From
this the value of $x + y$ cannot be determined.
For example, if $x = 9$ and $y = 1$, then all
4 percentages in the Venn diagram are
between 0 and 100, $9y = x$, and $x + y = 10$.
However, if $x = 18$ and $y = 2$, then all
4 percentages in the Venn diagram are
between 0 and 100, $9y = x$, and $x + y = 20$;
NOT sufficient.

Given both (1) and (2), it follows that $x = 45$
and $9y = x$. Therefore, $9y = 45$, or $y = 5$, and hence
$x + y = 45 + 5 = 50$.

**The correct answer is C;
both statements together are sufficient.**

71. A tank containing water started to leak. Did the tank contain more than 30 gallons of water when it started to leak? (Note: 1 gallon = 128 ounces)

    (1) The water leaked from the tank at a constant rate of 6.4 ounces per minute.

    (2) The tank became empty less than 12 hours after it started to leak.

**Arithmetic Rate Problems**

(1) Given that the water leaked from the tank at a constant rate of 6.4 ounces per minute, it is not possible to determine if the tank leaked more than 30 gallons of water. In fact, any nonzero amount of water leaking from the tank is consistent with a leakage rate of 6.4 ounces per minute, since nothing can be determined about the amount of time the water was leaking from the tank; NOT sufficient.

(2) Given that the tank became empty in less than 12 hours, it is not possible to determine if the tank leaked more than 30 gallons of water because the rate at which water leaked from the tank is unknown. For example, the tank could have originally contained 1 gallon of water that emptied in exactly 10 hours or the tank could have originally contained 31 gallons of water that emptied in exactly 10 hours; NOT sufficient.

Given (1) and (2) together, the tank emptied at a constant rate of

$$\left(6.4 \frac{\text{oz}}{\text{min}}\right)\left(60 \frac{\text{min}}{\text{hr}}\right)\left(\frac{1}{128} \frac{\text{gal}}{\text{oz}}\right) = \frac{(64)(6)}{128} \frac{\text{gal}}{\text{hr}} =$$

$$\frac{(64)(6)}{(64)(2)} \frac{\text{gal}}{\text{hr}} = 3 \frac{\text{gal}}{\text{hr}}$$ for less than 12 hours.

If $t$ is the total number of hours the water leaked from the tank, then the total amount of water emptied from the tank, in gallons, is $3t$, which is therefore less than $(3)(12) = 36$. From this it is not possible to determine if the tank originally contained more than 30 gallons of water. For example, if the tank leaked water for a total of 11 hours, then the tank originally contained $(3)(11)$ gallons of water, which is more than 30 gallons of water. However, if the tank leaked water for a total of 2 hours, then the tank

originally contained $(3)(2)$ gallons of water, which is not more than 30 gallons of water.

**The correct answer is E; both statements together are still not sufficient.**

72. Each of the 45 books on a shelf is written either in English or in Spanish, and each of the books is either a hardcover book or a paperback. If a book is to be selected at random from the books on the shelf, is the probability less than $\frac{1}{2}$ that the book selected will be a paperback written in Spanish?

    (1) Of the books on the shelf, 30 are paperbacks.

    (2) Of the books on the shelf, 15 are written in Spanish.

**Arithmetic Probability**

(1) This indicates that 30 of the 45 books are paperbacks. Of the 30 paperbacks, 25 could be written in Spanish. In this case, the probability of randomly selecting a paperback book written in Spanish is $\frac{25}{45} > \frac{1}{2}$. On the other hand, it is possible that only 5 of the paperback books are written in Spanish. In this case, the probability of randomly selecting a paperback book written in Spanish is $\frac{5}{45} < \frac{1}{2}$; NOT sufficient.

(2) This indicates that 15 of the books are written in Spanish. Then, at most 15 of the 45 books on the shelf are paperbacks written in Spanish, and the probability of randomly selecting a paperback book written in Spanish is at most $\frac{15}{45} < \frac{1}{2}$; SUFFICIENT.

**The correct answer is B; statement 2 alone is sufficient.**

73. A small school has three foreign language classes, one in French, one in Spanish, and one in German. How many of the 34 students enrolled in the Spanish class are also enrolled in the French class?

    (1) There are 27 students enrolled in the French class, and 49 students enrolled in either the French class, the Spanish class, or both of these classes.

(2)   One-half of the students enrolled in the Spanish class are enrolled in more than one foreign language class.

### Arithmetic Sets

Given that 34 students are enrolled in the Spanish class, how many students are enrolled in both the Spanish and French classes? In other words, given that $x + y = 34$ in the diagram below, what is the value of $y$?

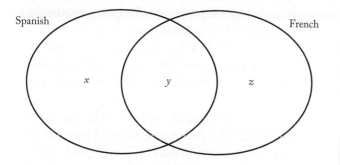

(1)   It is given that $y + z = 27$ and $x + y + z = 49$. Adding the equations $x + y = 34$ and $y + z = 27$ gives $x + 2y + z = 34 + 27 = 61$, or $y + (x + y + z) = 61$. Since $x + y + z = 49$, it follows that $y + 49 = 61$, or $y = 12$; SUFFICIENT.

(2)   Given that half the students enrolled in the Spanish class are enrolled in more than one foreign language class, then it is possible that no students are enrolled in the French and German classes only and 17 students are enrolled in both the Spanish and French classes. On the other hand, it is also possible that there are 17 students enrolled in the French and German classes only and no students enrolled in both the Spanish and French classes; NOT sufficient.

**The correct answer is A;
statement 1 alone is sufficient.**

74.   Last year $\frac{3}{5}$ of the members of a certain club were males. This year the members of the club include all the members from last year plus some new members. Is the fraction of the members of the club who are males greater this year than last year?

(1)   More than half of the new members are male.

(2)   The number of members of the club this year is $\frac{6}{5}$ the number of members last year.

### Arithmetic Operations with Fractions

Let $L$ represent the number of members last year; $N$ the number of new members added this year; and $x$ the number of members added this year who are males. It is given that $\frac{3}{5}$ of the members last year were males. It follows that the number of members who are male this year is $\frac{3}{5}L + x$. Also, the total number of members this year is $L + N$. Determine if $\dfrac{\frac{3}{5}L + x}{L + N} > \frac{3}{5}$, or equivalently, determine if $3L + 5x > 3L + 3N$ or simply if $x > \frac{3}{5}N$.

(1)   This indicates that $x > \frac{1}{2}N$. If, for example, $N = 20$ and $x = 11$, then $11 > \frac{1}{2}(20) = 10$, but $11 \not> \frac{3}{5}(20) = 12$. On the other hand, if $N = 20$ and $x = 16$, then $16 > \frac{1}{2}(20) = 10$, and $16 > \frac{3}{5}(20) = 12$; NOT sufficient.

(2)   This indicates that $L + N = \frac{6}{5}L$. It follows that $N = \frac{1}{5}L$. If, for example, $L = 100$, then $N = \frac{1}{5}(100) = 20$. If $x = 11$, then $11 \not> \frac{3}{5}(20) = 12$. On the other hand, if $x = 16$, then $16 > \frac{1}{2}(20) = 10$, and $16 > \frac{3}{5}(20) = 12$; NOT sufficient.

Taking (1) and (2) together is of no more help than (1) and (2) taken separately since the same examples were used to show that neither (1) nor (2) is sufficient.

**The correct answer is E;
both statements together are still not sufficient.**

75.   Machines K, M, and N, each working alone at its constant rate, produce 1 widget in x, y, and 2 minutes, respectively. If Machines K, M, and N work simultaneously at their respective constant rates, does it take them less than 1 hour to produce a total of 50 widgets?

(1)   $x < 1.5$

(2)   $y < 1.2$

**Algebra Work Problems**

Because Machine N produces 1 widget every 2 minutes, Machine N produces $\frac{60}{2} = 30$ widgets in 1 hour = 60 minutes.

(1) Given that $x < 1.5$, it follows that Machine K, which produces $\frac{60}{x} =$ widgets in 60 minutes, produces more than $\frac{60}{1.5} = 40$ widgets in 1 hour = 60 minutes. Thus, regardless of the number of widgets produced by Machine M, when all three machines are working simultaneously at their respective constant rates, more than $30 + 40 = 70$ widgets will be produced in 1 hour. Therefore, the three machines will together have produced 50 widgets in less than 1 hour; SUFFICIENT.

(2) Given that $y < 1.2$, it follows that Machine M, which produces $\frac{60}{y} =$ widgets in 60 minutes, produces more than $\frac{60}{1.2} = 50$ widgets in 1 hour = 60 minutes. Thus, regardless of the number of widgets produced by Machine K, when all three machines are working simultaneously at their respective constant rates, more than $30 + 50 = 80$ widgets will be produced in 1 hour. Therefore, the three machines will together have produced 50 widgets in less than 1 hour; SUFFICIENT.

**The correct answer is D;
each statement alone is sufficient.**

76. Stations X and Y are connected by two separate, straight, parallel rail lines that are 250 miles long. Train P and train Q simultaneously left Station X and Station Y, respectively, and each train traveled to the other's point of departure. The two trains passed each other after traveling for 2 hours. When the two trains passed, which train was nearer to its destination?

    (1) At the time when the two trains passed, train P had averaged a speed of 70 miles per hour.

    (2) Train Q averaged a speed of 55 miles per hour for the entire trip.

**Arithmetic Applied Problems; Rates**

(1) This indicates that Train P had traveled $2(70) = 140$ miles when it passed Train Q. It follows that Train P was $250 - 140 = 110$ miles from its destination and Train Q was 140 miles from its destination, which means that Train P was nearer to its destination when the trains passed each other; SUFFICIENT.

(2) This indicates that Train Q averaged a speed of 55 miles per hour for the entire trip, but no information is given about the speed of Train P. If Train Q traveled for 2 hours at an average speed of 55 miles per hour and Train P traveled for 2 hours at an average speed of 70 miles per hour, then Train P was nearer to its destination when the trains passed. However, if Train Q traveled for 2 hours at an average speed of 65 miles per hour and Train P traveled for 2 hours at an average speed of 60 miles per hour, then Train Q was nearer to its destination when the trains passed. Note that if Train Q traveled at $\frac{(120)(55)}{140} = 47\frac{1}{7}$ miles per hour for the remainder of the trip, then its average speed for the whole trip was 55 miles per hour; NOT sufficient.

**The correct answer is A;
statement 1 alone is sufficient.**

77. In a two-story apartment complex, each apartment on the upper floor rents for 75 percent as much as each apartment on the lower floor. If the total monthly rent is $15,300 when rent is collected on all of the apartments, what is the monthly rent on each apartment on the lower floor?

    (1) An apartment on the lower floor rents for $150 more per month than an apartment on the upper floor.

    (2) There are 6 more apartments on the upper floor than on the lower floor.

**Algebra Simultaneous Equations**

Let $x$ be the number of apartments on the lower floor, $y$ be the number of apartments on the upper floor, and $\$R$ be the monthly rent on each apartment on the lower floor. Then the monthly rent on each apartment on the upper floor is $0.75R$ and $Rx + 0.75Ry = 15{,}300$. Determine the value of $R$.

(1) Given that $R = 150 + 0.75R$, it follows that $0.25R = 150$, or $R = 600$; SUFFICIENT.

(2) Given that $y = x + 6$ thus, $Rx + 0.75R(x + 6) = 15{,}300$, or $1.75Rx + 4.5R = 15{,}300$, which can be true for more than one value of $R$ and a corresponding positive integer value of $x$. For example, it is possible that $R = 600$ and $x = 12$, and it is possible that $R = 425$ and $x = 18$; NOT sufficient.

**The correct answer is A; statement 1 alone is sufficient.**

78. A motorboat, which is set to travel at $k$ kilometers per hour in still water, travels directly up and down the center of a straight river so that the change in the boat's speed relative to the shore depends only on the speed and direction of the current. What is the value of $k$?

(1) It takes the same amount of time for the boat to travel 4 kilometers directly downstream as it takes for it to travel 3 kilometers directly upstream.

(2) The current flows directly downstream at a constant rate of 2.5 kilometers per hour.

### Algebra Applied Problems

Letting $c$ represent the speed of the current, the boat travels $(k + c)$ kilometers per hour (kph) when traveling in the same direction as the current (downstream) and $(k - c)$ kph when traveling in the opposite direction as the current. Determine the value of $k$.

(1) Given that it takes the same amount of time to travel 4 kilometers (km) downstream as it takes to travel 3 km upstream, it follows that $\dfrac{4}{k + c} = \dfrac{3}{k + c}$, or $k = 7c$, which shows that the value of $k$ depends on the value of $c$; NOT sufficient.

(2) Given that $c = 2.5$ kph, it is not possible to determine the value of $k$ since no information is given about the value of $k$ or its relationship with $c$; NOT sufficient.

Taking (1) and (2) together, $k = 7c = 7(2.5) = 17.5$.

**The correct answer is C; both statements together are sufficient.**

79. If the book value of a certain piece of equipment was $5,000 exactly 5 years ago, what is its present book value?

(1) From the time the piece of equipment was purchased, its book value decreased by 10 percent of its purchase price each year of its life.

(2) The present book value of another piece of equipment is $2,000.

### Algebra Applied Problems

Determine the present book value of a piece of equipment, of which the book value exactly 5 years ago was $5,000.

(1) Given that the book value decreased 10% of the purchase price each year, it is not possible to determine the present book value because the purchase price is unknown as is the number of years ago the equipment was purchased. Consider the following chart, where $P$ represents the purchase price.

| Years after purchase | Depreciation | Book value |
| --- | --- | --- |
| 0 | 0 | $P$ |
| 1 | $0.1P$ | $0.9P$ |
| 2 | $0.1P$ | $0.8P$ |
| 3 | $0.1P$ | $0.7P$ |
| 4 | $0.1P$ | $0.6P$ |
| 5 | $0.1P$ | $0.5P$ |
| 6 | $0.1P$ | $0.4P$ |
| 7 | $0.1P$ | $0.3P$ |
| 8 | $0.1P$ | $0.2P$ |
| 9 | $0.1P$ | $0.1P$ |
| 10 | $0.1P$ | 0 |
| 11 | 0 | 0 |
| 12 | 0 | 0 |
| 13 | 0 | 0 |

For example, if "5 years ago" was 6 years after purchase and the book value was $5,000, then $5{,}000 = 0.4P$ and

$P$ = $12,500. In this case, the present book value (i.e., 5 years hence) is $0. On the other hand, if "5 years ago" was 2 years after purchase and the book value was $5,000, then $5,000 = 0.8$P$ and $P$ = $6,250. In this case, the present book value (i.e., 5 years hence) is 0.3($6,250) = $1,875; NOT sufficient.

(2) Given that the present book value of another piece of equipment is $2,000 gives no information about the certain piece of equipment under consideration; NOT sufficient.

Taking (1) and (2) together gives no more information than (1) alone since (2) gives information about another piece of equipment, not the piece under consideration.

**The correct answer is E; both statements together are not sufficient.**

80. The total cost to charter a bus was shared equally by the people who went on a certain trip. If the total cost to charter the bus was $360, how many people went on the trip?

(1) Each person who went on the trip paid $9 to charter the bus.

(2) If 4 fewer people had gone on the trip, each person's share of the total cost to charter the bus would have increased by $1.

**Algebra First-Degree Equations**

Let $n$ be the number of people who went on the trip and $p$ be the amount that each person paid. Then $np$ = 360. What is the value of $n$?

(1) Given that $p$ = 9, then $9n$ = 360, or $n$ = 40; SUFFICIENT.

(2) Given that $(n - 4)(p + 1)$ = 360, or $np + n - 4p - 4$ = 360, it follows from $np$ = 360 that $n - 4p - 4$ = 0. Multiplying both sides of this last equation by $n$ gives $n^2 - 4np - 4n$ = 0, or $n^2 - 4(360) - 4n$ = 0, or $n^2 - 4n - 1,440$ = 0. Factoring gives $(n - 40)(n + 36)$ = 0, and hence $n$ = 40 since $n$ is a positive integer; SUFFICIENT.

**The correct answer is D; each statement alone is sufficient.**

81. If each of the stamps Carla bought cost 20, 25, or 30 cents and she bought at least one of each denomination, what is the number of 25-cent stamps that she bought?

(1) She spent a total of $1.45 for stamps.

(2) She bought exactly 6 stamps.

**Arithmetic Applied Problems**

Let $x$, $y$, and $z$ be the number of 20, 25, and 30 cent stamps, respectively, that Carla bought. What is the value of $y$?

(1) Given that $20x + 25y + 30z$ = 145, it is not possible to determine the value of $y$. For example, if $x$ = 3, $y$ = 1, and $z$ = 2, then each of $x$, $y$, and $z$ is a positive integer and $20x + 25y + 30z$ = 145. However, if $x$ = 2, $y$ = 3, and $z$ = 1, then each of $x$, $y$, and $z$ is a positive integer and $20x + 25y + 30z$ = 145; NOT sufficient.

(2) Given that $x + y + z$ = 6, it is not possible to determine the value of $y$, because each the two examples used in (1) satisfies $x + y + z$ = 6; NOT sufficient.

Taking (1) and (2) together, it is not possible to determine the value of $y$ because the two examples above each satisfy both (1) and (2).

**The correct answer is E; both statements together are still not sufficient.**

82. A car traveled a distance of $d$ miles in $t$ minutes at an average rate of $r$ miles per minute. What is the ratio of $d$ to $r$?

(1) $t$ = 30

(2) $d$ = 25

**Algebra Applied Problems**

Determine the ratio of $d$ to $r$ for a car that traveled $d$ miles in $t$ minutes at an average rate of $r$ miles per minute. Note that since $d = rt$ and $\frac{d}{r} = t$, determining the ratio of $d$ to $r$ amounts to determining $t$.

(1) Given that $t$ = 30, it follows that $\frac{d}{r}$ = 30; SUFFICIENT.

(2) Given that $d$ = 25, it is not possible to determine the ratio of $d$ to $r$ since no information is given about the value of $r$ nor

is information given from which to obtain the value of $r$; NOT sufficient.

**The correct answer is A;
statement 1 alone is sufficient.**

83. Pat is reading a book that has a total of 15 chapters. Has Pat read at least $\frac{1}{3}$ of the pages in the book?

    (1) Pat has just finished reading the first 5 chapters.

    (2) Each of the first 3 chapters has more pages than each of the other 12 chapters in the book.

**Arithmetic Applied Problems**

Determine if Pat has read at least $\frac{1}{3}$ of the pages in a 15-chapter book.

(1) Given that Pat has just finished reading the first 5 chapters in the book, she may or may not have read $\frac{1}{3}$ of the pages in the book. If the first 5 chapters were very short and she has read no other pages in the book, it is possible that she has read less than $\frac{1}{3}$ of the pages in the book. If the first 5 chapters were very long and/or she has read other pages in the book, it is possible that she

has read at least $\frac{1}{3}$ of the pages in the book; NOT sufficient.

(2) Given that each of the first 3 chapters has more pages than each of the other 12 chapters, it is impossible to determine whether Pat has read at least $\frac{1}{3}$ of the pages in the book because information is not given about how many chapters or which chapters of the book Pat has read; NOT sufficient.

Taking (1) and (2) together, if Pat has read just the first 5 chapters and each of the first 3 chapters has 10 pages, each of chapters 4 and 5 has 1 page, and each of the other 10 chapters has 9 pages, then Pat has read 32 pages of the book, which has $32 + 90 = 122$ pages and $\frac{32}{122} < \frac{1}{3}$. On the other hand, if Pat has read at least the first 5 chapters, each of the first 3 chapters has 10 pages and each of the other 12 chapters has 9 pages, then Pat has read at least 48 pages of the book, which has $48 + 90 = 138$ pages and $\frac{48}{138} > \frac{1}{3}$.

**The correct answer is E;
both statements together are still not sufficient.**

# 6.0 GMAT™ Official Guide Data Insights Review Question Index

# 6.0 GMAT™ Official Guide Data Insights Review Question Index

The Data Insights Review Question Index is organized by GMAT™ section, difficulty level, and then by mathematical concept. The question number, page number, and answer explanation page number are listed so that questions within the book can be quickly located.

## Data Insights – Chapter 5 – Page 90

| Difficulty | Concept | Question # | Page | Answer Explanation Page |
|---|---|---|---|---|
| Easy | Applied Problems | 3 | 102 | 114 |
| Easy | Applied Problems | 8 | 103 | 116 |
| Easy | Applied Problems | 9 | 103 | 116 |
| Easy | Applied Problems | 10 | 103 | 116 |
| Easy | Applied Problems | 12 | 103 | 117 |
| Easy | Applied Problems | 14 | 103 | 118 |
| Easy | Applied Problems | 24 | 104 | 122 |
| Easy | Applied Problems | 27 | 105 | 124 |
| Easy | Applied Problems | 29 | 105 | 125 |
| Easy | First-Degree Equations | 4 | 102 | 114 |
| Easy | First-Degree Equations | 16 | 103 | 119 |
| Easy | First-Degree Equations | 19 | 104 | 120 |
| Easy | Inequalities | 26 | 104 | 123 |
| Easy | Percents | 13 | 103 | 118 |
| Easy | Percents | 20 | 104 | 121 |
| Easy | Percents | 22 | 104 | 122 |
| Easy | Percents | 30 | 105 | 125 |
| Easy | Probability | 2 | 102 | 113 |
| Easy | Rate Problems | 11 | 103 | 117 |
| Easy | Ratio and Proportion; First-Degree Equations | 23 | 104 | 122 |
| Easy | Series and Sequences | 25 | 104 | 123 |

*(Continued)*

| Difficulty | Concept | Question # | Page | Answer Explanation Page |
|---|---|---|---|---|
| Easy | Simultaneous Equations | 18 | 104 | 120 |
| Easy | Statistics | 1 | 102 | 113 |
| Easy | Statistics | 5 | 102 | 114 |
| Easy | Statistics | 6 | 102 | 115 |
| Easy | Statistics | 7 | 103 | 115 |
| Easy | Statistics | 15 | 103 | 118 |
| Easy | Statistics | 17 | 104 | 119 |
| Easy | Statistics | 21 | 104 | 121 |
| Easy | Statistics | 28 | 105 | 124 |
| Easy | Statistics | 31 | 105 | 125 |
| Medium | Applied Problems | 34 | 105 | 127 |
| Medium | Applied Problems | 35 | 106 | 128 |
| Medium | Applied Problems | 36 | 106 | 128 |
| Medium | Applied Problems | 38 | 106 | 129 |
| Medium | Applied Problems | 40 | 106 | 130 |
| Medium | Applied Problems | 41 | 106 | 131 |
| Medium | Applied Problems | 54 | 108 | 137 |
| Medium | Applied Problems | 56 | 108 | 137 |
| Medium | Applied Problems | 58 | 108 | 138 |
| Medium | Estimation | 33 | 105 | 127 |
| Medium | First-Degree Equations | 49 | 107 | 135 |
| Medium | Interpretation of Tables; Sets (Venn Diagrams) | 32 | 105 | 126 |
| Medium | Percents | 43 | 106 | 132 |
| Medium | Percents | 48 | 107 | 134 |
| Medium | Percents | 53 | 108 | 136 |
| Medium | Probability | 46 | 107 | 133 |
| Medium | Ratio and Proportion | 37 | 106 | 128 |
| Medium | Simultaneous Equations | 39 | 106 | 129 |
| Medium | Simultaneous Equations | 47 | 107 | 134 |

*(Continued)*

| Difficulty | Concept | Question # | Page | Answer Explanation Page |
|---|---|---|---|---|
| Hard | Sets | 73 | 110 | 144 |
| Hard | Simultaneous Equations | 61 | 109 | 139 |
| Hard | Simultaneous Equations | 77 | 110 | 146 |
| Hard | Work Problems | 75 | 110 | 145 |

# Appendix A   Answer Sheet

# Data Insights Answer Sheet

| | | | |
|---|---|---|---|
| 1. | 18. | 35. | 52. | 69. |
| 2. | 19. | 36. | 53. | 70. |
| 3. | 20. | 37. | 54. | 71. |
| 4. | 21. | 38. | 55. | 72. |
| 5. | 22. | 39. | 56. | 73. |
| 6. | 23. | 40. | 57. | 74. |
| 7. | 24. | 41. | 58. | 75. |
| 8. | 25. | 42. | 59. | 76. |
| 9. | 26. | 43. | 60. | 77. |
| 10. | 27. | 44. | 61. | 78. |
| 11. | 28. | 45. | 62. | 79. |
| 12. | 29. | 46. | 63. | 80. |
| 13. | 30. | 47. | 64. | 81. |
| 14. | 31. | 48. | 65. | 82. |
| 15. | 32. | 49. | 66. | 83. |
| 16. | 33. | 50. | 67. | |
| 17. | 34. | 51. | 68. | |

**Notes**

# Notes

# Notes

**Focus Edition**

# Power Up Your Prep with Official Practice Exams

Research shows that first-time GMAT test takers can **increase their scores by up to 75 points** after taking all Official Practice Exams!

## Benefit from:

- ◎ The same scoring algorithm as the real GMAT Focus, with questions that adapt in difficulty as you improve

- ◎ Scaled section scores and a total score that aligns to the actual test

- ◎ Detailed score performance report, including time management

**Get your Official Practice at mba.com/gmatprep**